FLOATING IN QUIET DARKNESS

HOW THE FLOATATION TANK HAS CHANGED OUR LIVES AND IS CHANGING THE WORLD

Samadhi Tank II

i

Floating in Quiet Darkness
How the Floatation Tank Has Changed Our Lives and Is Changing the World

First Trade Edition
Cover art by Lill McGill
Cover design by Gailyn Porter
Layout by Gailyn Porter
Editing by Laurie Arroyo and Iven Lourie

Trade Paperback ISBN: 978-0-89556-292-0
PDF ISBN: 978-0-89556-638-6
MobiPocket ISBN: 978-0-89556-637-9
EPUB ISBN: 978-0-89556-639-3

Published by:
Gateways Books & Tapes / I.D.H.H.B., Inc.
P.O. Box 370
Nevada City, California 95959
(530) 271-2239 or (800) 869-0658
info@gatewaysbooksandtapes.com

Library of Congress Cataloging-in-Publication Data

Names: Perry, Lee (Perry's Samadhi Tanks), author. | Perry, Glenn, 1941-
   author.
Title: Floating in quiet darkness : how the floatation tank has changed our
   lives and is changing the world / by Lee and Glenn Perry.
Description: First Trade edition. | Nevada City, California : Gateways
   Books and Tapes, 2021. | Includes bibliographical references.
Identifiers: LCCN 2020049823 (print) | LCCN 2020049824 (ebook) | ISBN
   9780895562920 (trade paperback) | ISBN 9780895566386 (pdf) | ISBN
   9780895566393 (epub) | ISBN 9780895566379 (mobi)
Subjects: LCSH: Sensory deprivation--Therapeutic use. | Altered states of
   consciousness.
Classification: LCC RC489.S44 P47 2021 (print) | LCC RC489.S44 (ebook) |
   DDC 616.89/14--dc23
LC record available at https://lccn.loc.gov/2020049823
LC ebook record available at https://lccn.loc.gov/2020049824

We dedicate this book to
Dr. John C. Lilly
who supported us in our life of service
with the Samadhi Tank Company
and inspired us to devote our lives
to expanding consciousness.

TABLE OF CONTENTS

Samadhi Philosophy

We recognize our obligation to make ourselves available to people after their use of the tank, whether we provide silence, another appointment, good listening and good responding, or something we haven't thought of. We are there to listen and help them explore their experience, if that's what they're interested in doing. We realize that we best serve our customers and ourselves by reflecting truthfully, in our own behavior, the fundamental, positive qualities of the tank experience itself. Our job is to remain open-minded, unbiased, centered, supportive, relaxed, personally responsible and energetically aware. Really working in this way keeps our work a source of personal growth and evolution.

The tank is a general-purpose tool, not a design for something in particular. It is nothing and it is a powerful instrument for change. It is an environment for learning about oneself, in whatever way one wishes, without distraction. It does not tell us what to do, and neither should we presume to tell others what their experience should be, either before or after their float. We trust in the inherent capacity of the individual to discover what is best for themselves. We believe that the most effective experience occurs when initiative and power is left with the person and we are there to encourage that. After floating, people are often in the present moment, and emit the glow of present time unfolding, a sense of peace and wellbeing. When we welcome this state, it may be eager to make a return visit on following floats.

Acknowledgements

We have been working on this book for more than two years, and for a lifetime. We have many to thank for their contributions to our lives and this book.

First, we want to thank the miracles that are our children, who offered themselves with open hearts layered in love. The youngest, Josh, helped us on the business side. In his work as a management consultant he shared his understanding of many facets of the business world, including financial modeling and the alignment of goals. At the last minute he also did an edit and helped craft a piece describing the state of the industry now. In the middle, Shoshana has been working with Samadhi for most of her adult life. She lived in Italy in the 1980s and 90s where she played a major role in developing the worldwide market for floating, and, more recently, she played a substantial role in working with health departments to develop sanitation standards for the industry. Her support of Samadhi over the years has been invaluable.

When the eldest, Laurie, joined us to work on the book, by telephone, using Google Docs, in the midst of the coronavirus pandemic, it was understood that we both wished for her to help us with our wording. If we did not like proposed changes, it was always easy to say so. She never took offense. She was so good at taking my convoluted sentences, rearranging them, and turning them into something clear. Often the three of us could work on a sentence for quite a while. After suggesting more than a dozen possibilities one of us would offer a suggestion that we all knew was perfect. I sometimes wondered if the book was already written somewhere in the Universe, and we just had to discover it.

When she comes across a piece that she feels needs improvement, there is a little pause which I grew to appreciate as her working on what to say without creating an upset. Then she is able to tell us what she thinks without us feeling put down.

The most incredible part of her work was how she was able to stay empty like the tank. She had no agenda other than supporting us having the best book, with Lee's and my visions presented in the best possible way. She always left herself and her ideas and points of view out of the process. Sometimes, when Lee and I were trying to come up with what we wanted to say, the three of us would be quiet for more than a minute. Lee and I would then work together on what to say and Laurie would simply wait, patiently. Most people would have started to offer help. She never, ever did that. We were so blessed to not have her distracting us or irritating us. Totally amazing.

Other times what she was reading was not sufficiently clear to her so she had to probe and explore to understand what we were trying to communicate. On several occasions she even helped us go deeper into an area to understand something about the situation that was actually new to us. I do not feel this quite communicates the enormity of her contribution because I think she can walk on water. See, if I say how great she is, it is not really understandable.

This whole approach to working with us was a total reflection of how we work with a floater coming out of a tank. No personal agenda, no editorializing, no trying to help and no showing how smart we are, simply being empty like the tank.

The book is five or ten times as good as it otherwise would be. She is not perfect. If there are parts that are not great they are our creation and she could not correct everything.

They all have our utmost love and gratitude.

EJ Gold contributed an amazing amount to our understanding of consciousness, spirituality, and life in general. His community is always totally supportive.

Doug Mitchell, through his work with us, helped us to become more present, creative and connected to spirit.

Iven Lourie, besides editing, managed the entire publishing project, and Gailyn Porter did exceptional work with the aesthetics and layout.

Walli Ziegenhagen and Matthias Schossig, our best friends, were a sounding board during the creation of this book and beyond. For many years Walli was head of Samadhi production, and took charge of tending the vegetables and poultry we consumed.

Over many years Dan Weinberg has been our go-to I.T. guy, available around the clock, making sure our computers function well, and has continually helped with tank design and service.

Claude Needham has over the years made our website like the tank, simple, without distraction, far from the typical busy aesthetic of most modern websites.

David Franco for constant help with the business part of the Samadhi Tank Co.

Dave Fowler made improvements in the consciousness chapter especially to the baby-walking story.

Special thanks to the story contributors who have allowed people to appreciate the depth and breadth of floating.

Jason McDonald for years has perceptively stated how different the tank is from pools or spas enormously helping the float industry.

Faustin Bray for constant support over the years.

Joan Perry for many kinds of support but especially with help writing.

Roselyn Gander for Proofreading

Dr. Alison Gopnik for her insight into children's consciousness and for my favorite sentence in the book. What to do if you want to understand what an expanded consciousness looks like as mentioned in chapter six.

Amber Magnolia Hill for wonderful help writing especially the chapter A Brief History of Names.

Annabelle Ziegenhagen for a relationship of love closest to a daughter to me.

There is no way I can tell my appreciation for everyone and a few more are: someone special unnamed, Joe Bilman, Monica Anton, Cliff and Marlene, Verd Nolan, Gary Abreim, Dan Rosenstein, Richard and Ali, John Turner, Tom Fine, Rod Punnett, Bob Tyhurst, Dick, Pat, Julia, Bill Perry, Stephen Johnson, Kevin Johnson, Lisa, Marney, Wren, the whole BD study group, the float community and especially the amazing Samadhi tank owners—we have had the best customers of any company.

We have been blessed by love and relationships with every single one of you.

Dr. John C. Lilly

Foreword by Dr. John C. Lilly*

It is with pleasure that I introduce this new book by two long-time associates of mine who are also two veterans—or I might say, survivors—of the now over twenty-year history of the floatation tank practice which I myself initiated. Glenn Perry attended some of my earliest workshops exploring the underwater environment and gestalt of the dolphin species. Along with Steve Conger, he was among the first to take my original modified laboratory equipment and refine the design to create a range of efficient and aesthetic tanks for home and experimental uses. In case it is not clear from Glenn and Lee's own book, I will state here that Glenn was and is a top-notch engineer and artisan whose tank designs transcend the ordinary. He and his wife, Lee, an admirable working dyad, have certainly left the realm of commercialism far behind in their consistent offering of tanks of superior quality and performance.

The Perrys' Samadhi Tanks are worthy of praise. Their marketing has also escaped the large morass of fantasies and misrepresentation in relation to exploration of consciousness so prevalent currently. There is something more that needs saying here about their way of working with floating over the years.

In my first publication of *The Deep Self*, the original book on the subject of floating, I quoted as an epigraph the following passage from earlier work, *Programming and Metaprogramming in the Human Biocomputer*:

To become impartial, dispassionate, and general purpose, objective, and open-ended, one must test and adjust the level of credence in each of his sets of beliefs. If every Man is to be faced with real organisms with greater wisdom, greater intellect, greater minds than any single man has, then we must be open, unbiased, sensitive, general purpose, and dispassionate. Our needs for phantasias must have been analyzed and seen for what they are and are not or we will be in even graver troubles than we are today.

Our search for mentally healthy paths to human progress in the innermost realities depends upon progress in this area. Many men have

---

*We have been planning on writing this book about our history starting the float industry and our relationship with Dr. Lilly for many years. In one of our conversations with John Lilly we talked with him about this idea. Much to our surprise and pleasure, he immediately honored us with this foreword for our planned book. Lee and Glenn *floundered in this area of belief; I hope this work can help to find a way through one of our stickiest intellectual-emotional regions.*

This is a statement I will stand by as a good opener for any book on the tank and the work involved with floating. As I have stated and written elsewhere, it is no longer possible for any human to have the tank experience that I had, i.e., floating in darkness and isolation with absolutely no prior conditioning regarding what one might sense and experience. I was able to approach floating with a purely experimental outlook, a hypothesis to prove or disprove, with no preliminary data weighing the issue one way or the other.

By this time, so many accounts have been published, so much research done, so many articles printed, so many citations in the literature, recorded interviews and lectures—not to mention movies and television—that it is hardly possible for a first-time floater to have no preconceived notions of the floating experience. I must personally take responsibility for a large part of this widely-circulating reportage. On the other hand, in a training situation, or in a public floatation tank facility, there is a great deal that can be done to minimize the effects of pre-programmed beliefs about the tank. Attitudes of the trainer or the tank center operator will have influence, and the degree of impartiality versus bias as modeled by the local space "authority" will inevitably produce expectations or beliefs for the novice.

This being the case, I would like to state for the record that Glenn and Lee Perry have my endorsement as researchers of the highest caliber in the study of belief systems. I know I can trust them never to unnecessarily influence other humans and that their approach to floating will always follow the guidelines of my own personal and professional researches in "alternity." I heartily recommend their practice of floating, their methods of exploration, their uses of the benign and highly beneficial technology I have pioneered. The balanced, scientific, and pristine nature of their practice has been clear to me for years and so, not only for their expertise and their ingenuity, their skill and aptitude in tank manufacture, but also and especially for their genuine integrity and sincerity in this research—I recommend to you the Perrys' book and the Perrys themselves.

John C. Lilly
September, 1992

FLOATING IN QUIET DARKNESS

HOW THE FLOATATION TANK HAS CHANGED OUR LIVES AND IS CHANGING THE WORLD

CHAPTER ONE

DR. JOHN C. LILLY,
OUR MENTOR

Glenn Perry, Lee Perry, John C. Lilly

Dr. John C. Lilly

In 1954, in an abandoned building constructed by the Navy during World War II to study the metabolism of underwater swimmers, a lanky 39-year-old donned breathing apparatus and slipped into the water of an eight-foot tank at the National Institutes of Health in Bethesda, Maryland. As he did so, he turned off the lights, his body slid down, then slowly floated to the surface and hung out there. And waited. He was wondering what was going to happen. He thought he might go to sleep. He did not. He hung out there for a while, and finally climbed out. He liked it so much he started using it frequently.

At sixteen John Lilly had posed the question, "Can the mind render itself sufficiently objective to study itself?" At 39, already established at the cutting edge of neurophysical research, this was the first time he had turned his expertise to studying the longstanding debate over what would happen to the brain in the relative absence of physical stimulation. Would it simply, as many theorized, go to sleep? Or is there some inherent mechanism, a pacemaker of "awakeness," whether or not the brain is conducting transactions with the external world?

His University of Pennsylvania training led him to look at the physics and biophysics of physical stimulation. He realized that, short of cutting the nerves going to the brain, to study the brain/mind relationship it was necessary to isolate the body from external stimuli. The easy ones were sound, light, and motion. More difficult was the effect of gravity: the stagnation of blood flow to the skin and muscles supporting whatever posture, evident by tossing and turning, shifting from foot to foot, and so on. Also difficult to control were temperature differences; the air flow over the body that cools those parts exposed to it. He came to visualize a light and sound proof, water-filled tank that, at the proper temperature, would have the added advantage of diffusing the heat generated within the body.

The availability of a tank for his 24-hour private use, with the precise temperature controls necessary for his purpose, was just one of Dr. Lilly's lifelong experiences with what he termed the Earth Coincidence Control Office (ECCO). Many people have lots of other names for this. He said ECCO determines the long term coincidences (synchronicity), those moments in the fabric of time when we suddenly and briefly become consciously aware that we have made a deeper connection with the universe or that which is greater than our individual self.

The first sessions in the tank were done at night. He had discovered that any serious scientific research he wanted to do needed to be done on his own time, uncontrolled by authorities. You did your other work, where you were paid, during the day. Then he started using this tank, floating, just about every lunch hour. When he got back to the office his secretary would wonder what he had been doing, returning with a smile and a bounce in his step. What could possibly have made him so energetic?

It later occurred to him that he could float with more buoyancy, that maybe he did not need the breathing apparatus. He used the tank with just twenty inches of water. He bent at the knees and did what he later referred to as dolphin breathing: inhaling and holding his breath until he needed to breathe again, and then exhaling and inhaling quickly so that his body didn't sink below the surface. To pursue this study of the mind/brain relationship required a distraction free environment which led John Lilly to invent the concept of the "isolation tank." It became a lab in which he could begin to understand the "being state." This reduced distraction environment allowed him to start meditation at the point that had previously only been achievable after much study. Undistracted in the tank, and with minimal training, he could begin concentrating immediately upon the inner perceptions and dive deep into his own mind.

Lee

For me, the temperature gradient changes on my skin can be a major source of distraction. By eliminating this, and reducing vision and hearing to the greatest extent possible, and floating at the surface with the gravitational field reduced to the minimum, as an experienced floater I can relax every single muscle. Even my ear muscles, my neck muscles, my hands, my arms, and my back. Finding the areas where I am holding tension, I let go to feel the nourishment of spending time outside my ordinary life.

In John Lilly's first three scientific papers on this work, published in 1956, 1957 and 1958, he found he could relax his mind and dream, and his consciousness was always there, ready to take charge. He could choose to relax and let things happen, in which case the images would free-associate, moving as if randomly from one to the next. Or he could choose to program what would happen, in a process similar to lucid dreaming, but with an even greater degree of control. He could invent a scenario ahead of time with his consciousness fully focused, and then relax and let his brain carry out the program. He found that the brain does not shut down. Indeed, the isolated mind is highly active and creative.

John Lilly, a man who cherished word play, at first called the tank his "Isolation - Solitude - Confinement - Happiness - Freedom - Domain" while his colleagues referred to it as "Sensory Deprivation." Their belief system made it impossible for them to appreciate his invention as they found "Sensory Deprivation" something to be feared and avoided while he found it to be a misnomer. This domain was a vast and rich source of new experience, an "inperience." Experiencing that his discoveries/revelations/insights were often found too revolutionary for the scientific establishment in which he worked, he refrained from sharing with his colleagues.

One of the reasons it is so hard to describe the floating experience is that when we are floating, that experience is the reality. When we want to put it into words, we must come into our ordinary state in which that experience does not exist. Because ordinary words cannot capture the experience, we provide the tank to "allow" people to explore and discover, to find out for themselves. In his 1982 *The Book of Floating*, Michael Hutchison referred to the floatation tank as a new tool with the potential to fundamentally change our relationships with our own selves and, thus, with our community, and with our greater world.

John C. Lilly discussing tank requirements with Glenn Perry

Glenn

When I first met Dr. Lilly I was a systems computer programmer helping create a time-sharing system at Scientific Data Systems, a mainframe computer manufacturer. John Lilly's far ranging intellect and imaginative mind formulated the analogy between people's nervous systems and computer programs, with our behaviors programmed by previous life events. He saw the structure of our nervous system as an evolution from simpler organisms. From our genetic codes to our fight-or-flight response, none of us can escape our own nature as programmable entities.

Each of us may literally be no more than the sum of our limited set of programs, whatever we believe. The survival of our species is dependent upon each of us transcending our beliefs. As in many spiritual disciplines, we must become the consciousness that is able to look at beliefs and disentangle ourselves from them to experience the universe anew.

For me, because of my work with computers, John's formulations had a special attraction. I came with a scientific mind. "It is only real if you can touch it, observe it and measure it." I was familiar with the physical and mental universes. It had not occurred to me to investigate my own consciousness; to study something outside the consensus reality of the time, which had already been deeply investigated by Eastern spiritual seekers. John's early investigation of spiritual matters provided many Westerners a special glimpse into an area most of us knew little about. Still to this day, for those of us who are pursuing floating in the tank, learning about John Lilly's use of isolation to increase consciousness can be especially transformative.

He was a physicist, M.D., psychiatrist, sailor, pilot, ham radio operator and computer expert. He has been described as "a walking syllabus of Western Civilization." Whale researcher Scott McVay goes even further, saying: "There was Kepler, Galileo, Newton, Einstein and then…Lilly. Certainly, his discovery of the dolphin's conscious breathing, their brain size and complexity, and his recognition of their intelligence and sentience was a major revelation." Dr. Lilly was the first scientist to explore communication with the aliens of the ocean we call cetaceans. [Editor's Note: Gateways Books and Tapes has reprinted Lilly's scientific classic *Mind of the Dolphin* in a contemporary paperback edition.]

Lee

John Lilly was a full-time explorer. In connection with his training in psychoanalysis at the University of Pennsylvania, he spent five years in daily psychoanalysis. Later he made use of Rolfing, homeopathy, acupuncture, meditation and, of course, floating. He became intentional, non-habitual and non-judgmental. He was not a drinker; he was not a pothead. He was always looking for a new opening, a new expansion, some way he could feel more, experience more, learn more, share more. More consciousness, more neurons, more things that stimulated him rather than inebriated him. John Lilly is as difficult to pin down as his reputation.

Some John Lilly aphorisms:
   Insanity/outsanity/unsanity
   Alternity
   Where there's a will, there's a won't.
   Why did 6 screw 7? Cause 7 8 9.

The province of the mind has no limits, no fixed point of view.
Simply "having in mind" is what one needs to figure things
out.
Nothing's wrong with beliefs, but being able to change them is
important.
Expect a Guru, he plays the FOOL; Expect a Zombie, he
displays Genius.
Stop avoiding the void—Get nothing from Samadhi

I had never met anyone like him! He observed himself rather
than others as he investigated consciousness and the thinking
process. He had no interest in small talk. He asked questions to
solve problems. At the beginning of our work together, we were
especially careful with our questions so we would not look stupid.
As we learned, we did not have to worry, he did not answer anything
stupid, actually. What he did was train us to ask questions and to
explore from numerous perspectives. I have tremendous respect
for him and the discipline he
brought to his work.

John and Toni Lilly

Colonel Alfred Merrill
Worden, NASA Apollo 15
lunar mission Endeavor pilot
and friend to Dr. Lilly, called
him one of the most original
creative thinkers he had
ever met, who struggled to
unveil the unknown mind in
the known brain. Dr. Lilly's
physician remarked with
awe that John Lilly was the only person he knew of whose least
accomplishment was becoming a medical doctor.

John Lilly's wife, Toni, used to tell a story about him that went
something like this:

*"There was this guy who came to the door saying he wanted to speak
with John. I checked with John who told me he was too busy. The guy
left. Two days later, there he was again. Repeat with John. Another two*

days and the determined fellow was back. I delivered the request. John was quiet, internal conversation in process. Then he looked at me and asked, 'Is he bigger than me?'" He agreed to see him.

Toni and John Lilly lived in a comfortable house in Decker Canyon, in the Malibu area, on a road winding a mile or two up from the Pacific Ocean. There was an avocado orchard planted by Toni for the fruit and to hide the house, which was set back, with several fences. There were no numbers and no name. To find the house you had to know where you were going. Once you got out of your car you

Toni Lilly

had to knock, yell, and wait for a response. Toni's office was in the front of the house where she could manage incoming traffic. John's area, with his books, papers and tank room, was in the rear, at the opposite end of the house. Upon entering, the main room was the large kitchen where you could often find Toni preparing foods from her native Sicily.

This was a house full of people talking, eating, coming and going. Outside the kitchen was a large room facing the hills where you could often see a quiet person sitting silently, getting up once in a while, going out the back door, maintaining a bubble around himself, or maybe going in and out onto a deck and disappearing once again. That was John at work.

In my early times with her, I put Toni on a pedestal and approached her with the insecurity and fears that often accompany relating to someone you believe holier than yourself. She would not have any of it. She spoke straight-forwardly, with nothing to hide or protect. Intimate feelings were delivered as reports, or learning possibilities. She moved quickly from teacher, to child, to grandmother, idea generator, confidante, friend, hostess…. You could not label her, not because she rejected labels, but because labels would not stick. When something/anything needed to be done, and someone walked by offering to do the job, it was theirs. Lucky for me, she was continually including more and new people in her work.

In February 1985 Toni invited me to accompany her on a trip to British Columbia, Canada. She and John were planning to go together, and he got sick at the last minute. Several of the people involved were in the floating world. I was thrilled to be invited. We made no formal plans about who would do what or when. We had early morning swims, attended the pre- arranged meetings, delivered impromptu speeches (she on the latest John Lilly events and me on the events in the float world), worked with video, and attended to special business as it presented itself. I was often shy making public presentations, and my shyness took a vacation. We were all connected with the worlds of consciousness and were pleased to share them. The trip was fruitful, easy and uncomplicated. It was a rare treat to have such a compatible traveling partner.

During the trip I took advantage of our time alone together to learn everything I possibly could about her thinking, and cooking. She was an excellent cook and throughout my life I often bonded with people over our shared interest in food. I started right in as soon as we were seated on the plane. My primary interest was in the thread that ran between the many different kinds of projects she and John had worked on. Toni told me that, in John's work, the "thread" had always been his interest in discovering the difference between the mind and the brain. All his work demonstrates this interest since his teenagery when he mapped positive and negative systems in the brain. Those systems which caused pain, fear, anxiety, and anger were called "negatively reinforcing" systems, "negative systems." Those which caused pleasure and positive motivations were called "positively reinforcing," "positive systems."

John was the first to use the computer analogy for the differences between hardware, the brain, and software, the mind. After being involved in many different projects, the ultimate question was always, "What is the difference between mind and brain, hardware and software?" The difference between John and Toni was the way they approached these things. Their training was quite different. His was in the sciences and hers in the arts. Over the centuries we have seen how this intersection between art and science can give rise to new ways of thinking about our world and the ways we interact with it. These two seemingly opposite disciplines, one compelled by boundless imagination, the other driven by methodical rigor, united in a shared curiosity to explore life's big questions, can result in a more complete understanding.

Faustin Bray has documented significant thought foundations of the scientific/poetic/ spiritual/technological cultural creatives of the late 20th century. In our conversation with her for this book, she told us that people referred to her as John's only student. These are some of the things Faustin told us about John Lilly and floating.

John used the tank to travel outside of his body, free from interruption, knowing he was in a safe space. He was happy to float at his home in Malibu with water from his well uncontaminated by fluoride or chlorine or other pollutants. The tank was important to John to remove all distractions. As a scientific observer, he found it a marvelous place to look at the chaos within himself without attributing it elsewhere.

John's curiosity about what the brain does under certain circumstances was enhanced by the permission that the environment of the tank allowed. John said there is no such thing as drugs, only chemicals. It is changing the molecular configuration within the brain itself that profoundly changes who you are, where you are going and where you came from. In experimenting with psychedelics, he was following J. B. S. Haldane who taught that you must be your own first subject. Faustin told us that as a kid, her mother left her to her own devices. When asked, her mother would say, "Let her alone, do not bug her, and don't do anything. Just let her alone."

John had all sorts of books and things around that offered a playground. *"It wasn't that he told me things. He just left stuff all over the place, and I gravitated to it. My mother had me looking at the stars and talking about UFOs, but John was the one that inspired going for it. I think everything he did, whether it was going deeper into refinement, and smaller and smaller, or larger and larger, out into space, he was navigating, and wanted to bring as many people along as possible.*

"For a long time, we were just playing around with food and seeing how different diets affected our consciousness. It was amazing: how I would feel, how much confidence I had. With certain diets, I would feel superhuman. On others, all I wanted to do was lie around on the lawn. He was constantly researching different effects on consciousness. He invited, but did not demand, exploring. John was the permissionary of all permissionaries."

To have this extraordinary scientist in the world of exploration into the unknown, Dr. Lilly, as our mentor, was an extraordinary stroke of luck. John Lilly led us on a journey to gather all the information we needed to supply an adult human with a private place that could hold water at a specific temperature, and have as many people in the world use the tank as possible in a distraction-free environment. His instructions were always: 1) Know where you are going; 2) Get started; 3) Always take the next step. Glenn improved the solution to make floating easy and certain, and designed the tank to be easily deliverable, affordable, and distraction-free. What emerged was a tool to allow the individual to be completely with themself, to find their own appreciation of what they would see.

Lee with John Lilly

CHAPTER TWO

FIRST FLOAT
AND GLENN'S AWAKENING

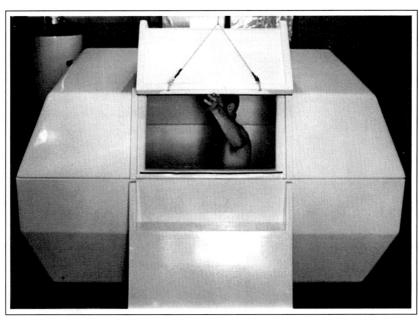

Fiberglass Prototype with Weight Assisted Door

Glenn's first prototype

Glenn

I spent the first eleven years of my life on the family fox farm in Cummington, a small town of about 200 people in western Massachusetts. Then, in 1953, we moved to Katonah, an upper class area 50 miles north of New York City where my father managed a herd of show cattle for a corporate lawyer on a good-sized estate. Half of the kids in the area went to prep school. The other half, in my public school, said I talked like a hick, like I had a hot potato in my mouth.

They called me Perry the fairy. I felt like the most persecuted kid in my class. In 1972, I had an experience that changed my life. I was a very shy, weird, nerdy kind of guy, working at Scientific Data Systems (SDS). All computers back then were huge mainframes that did batch processing. With batch processing, each user had sole control of the machine for a scheduled period of time. The user would arrive at the computer with program and data, often on punched paper cards and magnetic or paper tape, and execute the program. For example, for a business that needed weekly payroll, they would run that payroll. The next week they would come back with a new batch and produce that week's payroll.

Unlike other systems where you had to wait for your results, SDS's computers were unique in that they worked in real time. They did not do a batch once a week or anything like that. They calculated incoming data and sent results out to be used right then. If you wanted to control something you would get relatively immediate feedback to make modifications. This new kind of computer made things like space travel possible, by allowing for remote control in "real time." My work was on the project designing the first time-sharing system that allowed up to one hundred twenty-eight people, each on their own terminal connected by phone line, to interact with their own company computer as if they were the only one using it. This system and the computer were used at that time to explore the possibility of what is now known as the Internet.

At SDS we also used the timesharing system for our own work. In 1974, when I met Lee, I brought my terminal to her house and worked from there. I would dial the mainframe computer at SDS headquarters and work on it. On October 29, 1969, two of our computers, one at UCLA and the other at Stanford Research Institute, began a project funded by the U.S. Department of Defense, which believed it was important and valuable to have computers talking to each other.

The operators at UCLA sent the word "LOGON" to the SRI (Stanford) computer and called them up to make sure it was working.

The UCLA operator said, "I just sent an L. Did you get it?"

Stanford: "Yes"

UCLA: "O?"

Stanford: "Yes"

UCLA: "G?"

Stanford: "No, the darn thing just crashed."

That was the beginning of the Internet.

Back in 1972, my boss at SDS knew from our conversations that I was extremely interested in finding out how to improve the quality of my life. He suggested a recently published book, *The Center of the Cyclone*, by Dr. John Lilly. I read the book and was really impressed with this scientist/author who was talking about things that I found bizarre: consciousness and spirituality and changing your life. In my youth my family always went to church but, at that time and continuing to the present, I have not found spirituality in organized religion. I saw an ad for a week-long Dr. Lilly workshop. I signed up and went.

At the workshop location, there was a large flat-bottomed stone bowl cut from a mountain rock with a shack on top. We spent the first morning closing all the holes in the shack so that no light would penetrate. There were twenty inches of fresh water in the bowl. I was the first one in. I made it down the wooden ladder inside the shack and started kind of floating. I say "kind of" because although my head and torso were lying at the surface of the twenty inches of heated water, my legs were bent at the knees and my feet were flat on the bottom. I had been instructed to do "dolphin" breathing, which was taking a single inhale and, when I needed another breath, to exhale and inhale quickly, and hold it until I needed another breath, so as not to sink. John told us this is how dolphins breathe, that is, one breath at a time, swimming under the ocean surface until they need to take another breath. He had gotten rid of the breathing apparatus in his tank fairly early and done as I am describing for the past fifteen years. He would float in the twenty inches of water with his feet on the bottom and keep as much air in his lungs as possible by dolphin breathing, so he would not sink below the surface.

The area was a little larger than a bedroom with pillars supporting the shack above. I first spent a little time exploring. I used my feet to "walk" myself around the bowl, making sure not to hit my head on the edge of the bowl or on a pillar. It eventually became a little warm for me, but tolerable. I spent most of the time in my mind. At the end of an hour someone knocked to tell me time was up. When I came out it was as if the whole earth was a shimmering, shining, scintillating energy system, and time had slowed way down. I was in a totally different, unfamiliar state of consciousness. I slowly went to shower and experience this amazing universe.

We had lunch, and then John asked me to share my experiences, which I did comfortably. Well… at SDS if I went to the cafeteria with two people, I was too shy to open my mouth. The only way I would talk was if there was only one other person. Now, at this workshop, I was totally comfortable talking in front of a whole group of people. I thought: if something could make me able to open my mouth in front of a group of people—wow, it must be really incredible! This is what I had been looking for!! What a change in my consciousness.

I needed to build my own tank to use, a lot. By the end of the week, listening to other people's experiences and having more myself, I thought others would also want one. Since nobody was making them at the time, I should do it. After all, since I was making one for myself, with a little more energy I could easily make them for others. Boy, was I naive; it was a totally different thing making them commercially. If I had had any idea what I was getting myself into, my life might be an entirely different story. I asked John what he thought about the idea. He was excited. It supported his goal of having as many people as possible floating to raise consciousness in order to save our planet. John told me that it was most important to keep in mind that lack of distractions is what produces the impact of floating, the place you have always been looking for, the place of emptiness/nothingness, observing yourself in the universe. To develop the capacity for that sensitivity requires the maximum minimization of distractions. Distractions in the tank can be light, sound, temperature, gravity...

I lived upstairs in an apartment building near Venice Beach, California. I continued my day job at SDS and used my spare time to research making an isolation tank to give me a place to float weightless on the surface of skin temperature water while I did "dolphin breathing."

When I put an ear to any wall of my apartment and covered the other ear, I could hear indistinct mumbling from the people downstairs. From this I understood that sound could travel quite far through hard materials. People living near a loud street or a fire station or an airport would have a problem. I needed to solve how to keep all of that vibration from coming up through the bottom of the tank. At the workshop John had gone over with me different design considerations such as how to minimize distractions. Since I was intending to make a bunch of tanks for sale, I needed to be sure to have them work in any likely environment. I began in-depth research on the most effective approach to keeping distractions out, including light and sound.

I contacted a UCLA physics professor whose specialty was sound, and he took me first to an "anechoic" chamber and then to a "reverberation" room. The floor of the anechoic chamber was taut wire mesh suspended a few feet off the bottom surface. On the top, bottom and all four sides were thin foam wedges. The professor shot a .22 caliber blank pistol. The sound, like the small pop of uncorking champagne, went into the wedges and got lost bouncing back and forth between them until it lost energy. Next the professor shot the pistol in the reverberation room, made of six hard smooth surfaces. The sound was very loud and echoed, for, for, a, a, very, very, long, long, time, time, time, time....

Afterwards, the professor gave me information about how to keep sound from entering the tank. Without getting too technical, there are two kinds of sound reduction. The first is absorption, which the anechoic chamber is so good at, and which all noisy restaurants need. The second is a sound barrier to prevent sound or vibration from transferring from one space into another. For example, the front door of your house is good at keeping sound from coming into the house from the outside until you open the door a crack. When the tank is directly on the floor, structure-borne sound coming up through the bottom of the tank requires a barrier.

A good sound barrier is the interface of two mismatched materials. If you are at a swimming pool where a party is going on, and you put your head under water, the party sounds diminish greatly. The two mismatched materials are air and water. Their interface is an excellent mismatch. For structure-borne sound, layers of mismatched materials can be used between the tank and the floor. Absorptive materials like soft foam are not good sound barriers. They only prevent sound from reflecting; they do not prevent sound from passing through. This is why floatation tank center owners with open vessels in float rooms must spend a large amount of money making the rooms soundproof. [Editor's Note: More about tank and center design is covered in the Tank Design chapter.]

Light is a huge distraction and not easy to prevent. The structure of the tank needs to block light. I learned that vulnerable areas are around the door, and around any holes, such as where air enters and where any external filtration system connects. A structural material that is not black usually is not lightproof. Lots of seemingly likely materials are not. For example, very dark blue ABS plastic is not light proof, but black is, and therefore we have used it for our tanks. To prevent light from entering the tank through air holes requires dark non-reflective channels with numerous turns.

Temperature is even more difficult to address since people need slightly different temperatures to be comfortable. For example, I like the tank at one temperature and Lee likes it 0.75°F (.42°C) warmer. We used to put the tank temperature halfway between the two. At that temperature neither of us was comfortable. When it was .375°F (.21°C) above my ideal temperature I experienced it as too stuffy, like I did not have enough air. When Lee floated at the temperature .375°F (.21°C) too warm for me, she felt the tank was too cool. This definitely puts the lie to the term "sensory deprivation." If one must reference senses in the name of the device, then sensory enhancement would be much more appropriate.

In design, attention to small details can make all the difference.

Once I had researched removing distractions, I started designing and building a prototype, starting with the simplest four by four by eight-foot plywood box. The top had a cut one fourth of the way from the end, hinged to the rest of the top. Using my original float experience, I had a small ladder to get up and over the side. The prototype was coated with contact vinyl to combat the one hundred percent humid internal environment.

When John gave me the specifications for what the tank should be like, he mentioned that in the Virgin Islands he used ocean water to fill his tank. It was about three and a half percent salt and he thought I might want to add that much to my tank to float better. Perhaps due to his Rolfing, John had a very loose body that floated well. I had a very tight body that hardly floated. I put a lot more salt in the water so I could float without doing dolphin breathing and without having to support the lower part of my body with my feet on the bottom. Because of my poor ability to float, I had made a significant improvement to the tank design by adding enough salt to the water so I could float effortlessly.

After completing the design, I made and sold five to people I met around John. The humidity in the wooden environment became more of a concern. Even coating wood with something, such as polyester resin, it was not trivial to make a durable product. The polyester resin was toxic to use, and it made the product very heavy. I took a sculpture class at UCLA extension to learn more about design. I finally decided the tank needed to be made from plastic. After learning about different plastics and talking to my sculpture professor, I decided to make it out of fiberglass, despite the toxicity of the polyester resin. Intrigued, the professor was willing to design and build it for me.

I was very excited when it was finished, six months later, just in time to set up at a workshop at Esalen, a personal growth center 300 miles up the coast of California where John was giving a workshop. I put it on the top of my Oldsmobile and drove up the coast. After setting it up, getting the solution in and the filtration working, I turned on the temperature control system. Now I was free. I asked John if he minded if I dropped LSD. He said, "Don't involve me in that." He always thought people should take responsibility themselves for what they do.

A couple hours later John found me and let me know the tank was not heating up. He did not care that I was having trouble focusing. He expected me to change my state and become functional. A pang of fear shot through me. With all my will I wondered how to replace the heater. I suggested that one possibility was to go to the nearest town to find a store that sold them, but that would have to wait until the next day as it was now late afternoon.

He found that to be too uncertain and suggested we use a garden hose, submerging the middle of it in the solution as a radiator by trickling hot water through it, allowing the hot water to come out the end and go down the drain. Once every three sessions would be enough to keep it heated for the two days of the workshop. I found a groundskeeper who allowed us to borrow a hose for the duration of the workshop. I had survived the ordeal and learned that, with sufficient necessity, sometimes amazing things were possible.

When I returned to Los Angeles, I tested the heater which had been under the fiberglass tank bottom. It worked. It turned out there was an overload safety switch to shut it off when it got too hot. The thickness of the fiberglass had acted as a barrier, trapping the heat at its source, preventing it from dissipating into the solution. That was corrected by removing some of the

Amount of Epsom salt for ten inches of water

fiberglass and I gave the tank as a gift to John to use in his Malibu facility.

During that period, I was going to John Lilly workshops where we would investigate consciousness and reality. He gave seven workshops directed towards medical doctors because he thought they had the intelligence to appreciate his information about consciousness. I was lucky enough to be invited to all of those workshops. John thought they were important for my education. In these workshops I was exposed to different states of consciousness and to his way of approaching life and the world: To make as few assumptions as possible, to constantly observe oneself, and to question values. Most of us have difficulty seeing reality because we make assumptions rather than coming from "Beginner's Mind." When we observe ourselves it increases our awareness of ourselves and what we are doing.

In one exercise we paired up, sat facing each other, and focused on the other's third eye for half an hour. After about ten to fifteen minutes, my partner's appearance began changing: he was an old crony, a bird of prey, a strange hole. At the end we came together and shared our experiences. This altered my certainty of reality. Probably the most important effect I received from these workshops was to become dedicated to expanding my consciousness.

It was wonderful to float every day before work. On the way to work, where before I had been in the fast lane wondering why everyone was going so slow, now I was in the slow lane wondering why everyone was going so fast. Everything went a little easier. I did not get upset nearly as much, and I was a little happier. Life went better. Floating had already started to improve the quality of my life.

A Temporary Solution

The tank was becoming an integral part of my life and I needed to solve my design problems. I personally did not like fiberglass because it is very, very heavy. The door needed a weight on a pulley to make it light enough, or it needed air cylinders, which could fail. In addition, it was hard to make light proof, was expensive, required lots of labor and was toxic to fabricate. I didn't like plywood and I didn't like fiberglass so what could I do? Well, I did not have the slightest idea. I had a physics professor in college who said that there were two kinds of problems: simple ones and impossible ones. They were all impossible until you knew how to solve them, and then they were simple. This one was in the impossible category. Until I could find a suitable material for the structure, I decided to sell a tank kit. It included a temperature control system, filtration system, other materials including the liner, and instructions for making a plywood structure.

CHAPTER THREE

A BRIEF HISTORY OF NAMES

SENSORY DEPRIVATION
AND OTHER MISNOMERS

John Lilly signing tank

Lee and Glenn

Glenn

John Lilly's colleagues referred to his research as "Sensory Deprivation," which he found a total misnomer. In the mid 1980s Dr. Henry Adams, a dedicated scientific researcher in Reduced Environmental Stimulation Techniques (R.E.S.T.), and the well regarded peer-reviewed author of studies in substance abuse treatment, went on a largely successful campaign to remove the sensory deprivation moniker from the psychology textbooks and the float world. It reared its ugly head again around 2008 and continues through the printing of this book. Listening to your heart beat, muscles pop, eyelids blink, and taking the time and space to actually feel your breathing rise and fall—in all these ways and more a floatation tank deprives you of nothing except the distractions that prevent you from being with yourself.

In the early 1950s scientists at McGill University, under the direction of D.O. Hebb and funded by the Canadian Defense Research Board, began a series of experiments on what they labeled "sensory deprivation." The rationale given for the program at the time was to study hallucinatory perceptual phenomena experienced by people with monotonous jobs—radar observers, radio monitors, and truck drivers who commonly experienced sensory distortions.

In 1957 *Scientific American* wrote that the aim of this project was to obtain basic information about how humans would react in situations where nothing was happening. The purpose was not to cut individuals off from any sensory stimulation whatsoever, but to remove any meaning, so far as they could arrange it. However, it was later revealed that beneath the desire to study the phenomena was another motivation. There was a deep concern over the "confessions" being produced at the Russian Communist trials. They were actually conducting a secret study of brainwashing. They did not know what the Russian procedures were, but it seemed that they were producing some peculiar changes in attitude. How? It was theorized that a possible factor could be perceptual isolation so that is what they concentrated on.

John Lilly started a similar project independently with different techniques at the National Institutes of Mental Health. In the Canadian experiments, the aim was to reduce the patterning of stimuli to the lowest level; in his, the objective was to "reduce the absolute intensity of all exterior physical stimuli to the lowest possible level."

As Jack Vernon, a researcher who continued with sensory deprivation studies at Princeton, author of *Inside the Black Room: Studies of Sensory Deprivation*, points out, even in this extreme environment the term sensory deprivation is a misnomer. "Now obviously we did not, and could not, take entirely away the action of all the senses. It is possible to deprive the visual sense, totally extinguishing light, but it is not possible to do a similar thing with hearing. Even if a man is placed in a completely soundproof chamber, where no external sounds will reach him, he will still experience auditory sensations. He will hear blood coursing through those blood vessels that are near the ear. He will hear his breathing movements as well as occasional rumblings from the stomach, and the like. In addition to these, the mind also receives sensory stimulation that informs it of bodily movements, body positions, movements of muscles, changes in temperature, feelings of thirst and hunger, etc. Thus, it can be easily appreciated that to deprive a man totally of sensory stimulation would be a very difficult, if not impossible, task." Clearly the experience in the tank is not sensory deprivation, it is sensory enhancement, enhancing our capacity for sensitivity to ourselves. Removing the exterior distractions reveals how we distract ourselves. Floating in the tank, we observe who we are.

So if the term "sensory deprivation" isn't accurate when describing these early chamber experiments, how did it come to be associated with floatation tanks which had not even been invented when this research first took place? Films such as *The Manchurian Candidate* (1962), *The Mind Benders* (1963), and *Altered States* (1980) contributed to the use of this misnomer in popular culture. In addition, it was being used in basic college psychology textbooks.

As previously detailed, John Lilly's research method was to use himself as his first subject. In *The Deep Self* he suggests the term "sensory deprivation" was invented by those psychologists who did not research through self-investigation but experimented on subjects. Expecting a "deprivation state," the scientists contaminated their experiments. They did not find results, rather they created the results.

Lilly developed the idea of a tank filled with water with which to accomplish the reduction in intensity of physical stimuli, in response to the prevailing idea that consciousness was not primary but a result of interaction with the material world. The isolation tank was born.

Lilly soon realized the enormous potential of what he had created and started spending many hours in the tank as its benefits became more and more apparent. He started to call it an Isolation Tank in appreciation of the fact that it isolated the person from external distraction and allowed for a spacious inner solitude.

Lilly became interested in the subject of isolation in general after experiencing the benefits of his time in solitude, isolated from the constant demands of other people, sensory stimuli, and the effects of gravity. This line of inquiry led him to undertake a systematic study of the literature on the effects of extended periods of time spent alone due to traumatic and unusual situations such as shipwreck or accidents in extreme conditions in remote parts of the world. After reading numerous accounts of this kind, he concluded that physical dangers combined with solitude are extremely stressful. Isolation is a totally different experience for a person in a safe, relaxed environment than it is for someone in a stressful, dangerous environment (which many participants in Dr. Hebb's sensory deprivation chamber experiments felt they were in).

As Lilly points out (and an idea that would be a driving force throughout his life): isolation in a safe space allows one's consciousness to expand and explore anything the person can allow themselves to imagine, a powerful idea that has been corroborated by countless people since Lilly's time. The safety, isolation, and peace offered by the tank allow the mind the freedom to expand to unfathomable reaches of the conscious universe. Today, physicists have proven what ancient wisdom traditions have always said through their stories and mythology: consciousness is the primary force in the universe. John Lilly's isolation tank experiments confirmed this as well. Rather than the absence of external stimuli causing the inner awareness to go dormant, it allows for a vast opening of latent possibilities within each individual's consciousness. In the tank, isolation gives way to a boundless inner spaciousness.

As stated in Chapter One, I, a taciturn computer programmer working at Xerox in the 70s, took a workshop with John Lilly for five days near Big Bear, California, and got to try out a makeshift isolation tank. This first experience changed my life, and with John's blessing and mentorship, I became the first designer and manufacturer of tanks for the public.

I took what Lilly had learned over the years, added something new, and developed a tank design that would allow for commercial production so that others could have access to this experience. John had eventually realized he could make the tank even more distraction free by discarding the breathing apparatus. He kept his face above the water surface in order to breathe, lay on his back in twenty inches of water and bent his legs at the knees with his feet standing on the bottom so as not to sink below the surface. After breathing out, he needed to quickly breathe in so his head would not slip under the surface.

John switched from fresh water to ocean water in the tank when he moved to the Virgin Islands to study dolphins in the late 50s. When he first gave me guidance about designing the tank, he mentioned I could add three percent table salt (sodium chloride) to help me be more buoyant. Much less buoyant than he, I added enough salt that I could float without touching the bottom in just ten inches. When he tried it, he loved it. Then he suggested we up the salt to increase the density to twenty-five percent heavier than fresh water. When we reported to him that it was abrasive to the skin of some people, he suggested we switch to magnesium sulfate (Epsom salt) which was a good solution. By adding enough salt I had turned the isolation experience into a float experience. Lee and I then rechristened them "floatation tanks" as that was less threatening than "isolation tanks."

Since its invention the floatation tank has been a place to minimize the information coming into the senses, to be isolated from the stressors of the outside world, and to let us soar through our limitless consciousness.

CHAPTER FOUR
LEE'S INTRODUCTION TO FLOATING
THE TWO MEET
AND START A BUSINESS

We made it!

Lee and Glenn Perry

Lee

When I met Glenn, I was a widow with three grown kids (two of them still at home), a house, beginning my third year of teaching. During the previous five years I had immersed myself in the world of education. I was convinced there was a lot to be done in the educational system other than the ordinary practices of the day. My son had been a volunteer helper in the one-room, private parent-run school where I was teaching. He came home one day saying he had to stand in the corner of his public school seventh grade geography class for talking in the classroom without permission. I was reading voraciously about different ways and had removed my own kids from the regular schools to try different systems. They were interested in schools with different teacher/student relationships. My responsibilities were changing with my own children, and I was wondering what would happen next in my family. I was not sure it was my calling to teach, and I hung in there to find out.

I grew up on the streets of New York City where I learned to get along in lots of tough situations: subways, ghetto neighborhoods, and so on. It was not hard for me; it was home. I was not really tough myself. I liked people, all kinds of people. I knew how to listen and get along.

I ended up teaching at an "Inner City" school in Los Angeles. As in all big cities "Special Education" classes had the worst reputations: real tough work. I was one of the new teachers that year and was placed in **regular** fourth grade which was my favorite age class. The students had not yet entered puberty, were eager to learn and began to specialize in their favorite subject. Another (new to the school) teacher was hysterical after spending a few days with her new special education class. She begged to have someone take over for her. She could not handle it! She wept, pleaded....

I met the class, ten- to thirteen-year olds, Black and Chicano, bussed in from the poorest housing project in downtown Los Angeles fifteen minutes away. They were certified school failures, and they believed they were given the teachers who did not know how to teach. They had numerous strong complaints about: school, waiting for the bus, riding the bus, the other kids—skinny, fat, smart-ass, stupid—wrong language, reputations, muscle strength.

Everyone was busy blaming the next kid's mother many times daily as in "Your Mother, ..." She was BAD and treated you as best she could. The assigned teacher was unable to be in that classroom. She was crumbling into fear. I understood. I was touched, and I said I would switch with her.

The principal let me know that my main requirement was to keep these eighteen students out of his office. If I could do this, I was allowed to put them into my van and go to the park as often as we wanted. We got to know each other out of the school setting as well as in the classroom, and that increased the trust between us. This experience was HUGE. I got to know and be known by a real tough bunch of kids. I learned a lot, and maybe the kids did too. Just one example was the Thanksgiving celebration that is practiced in many L.A. elementary schools, where each class presents something outside of the curriculum that they have learned to perform. I thought I would try doing something with music because the kids were attracted to it, liked it, and did not get a chance to produce it at home in that pre-consumer-electronics age. The kids were enthusiastic. They knew Jingle Bells and could sort of sing it. We took our turn in the auditorium in the time we were given. I remember feeling incredibly nervous, more worried than they were. It was interesting to see and hear how well they did, how they came together, and how good they felt about it. It was the learning hit of the year!

Back to the "Isolation Tank"

I was a subject in an "Isolation Tank" research project. It was held in a two-car garage in a residential neighborhood. Vance, the interviewer, introduced me to the tank and gave me the instructions I was to follow. It was a rectangular wooden box, four by four by eight feet in size. I had to climb a small stepladder and drop down into a foot of lukewarm water with so much salt dissolved in it that I floated when I lay down on my back. My face and the top of my body were out of the solution, floating.

It was completely dark. Totally! I was still for a while. I really liked being buoyant. I stretched so my feet and arms could touch the walls. I had a small cut on my left shoulder that stung a little.

I got quiet, crossed my hands over my chest, and was comfortable. I remember telling myself, "I am here to help myself with my classroom problems." I thought my class would like the story of this adventure. I thought about how obsessed I was with learning. The kids were afraid they could not learn. I remember that feeling of fear about not learning. And then I understood how for many, school is a place about failing.

Vance gave me several tests when I got out of the isolation tank, congratulated me on how well I did, and invited me to a party at the house of the person who made the tank, Glenn Perry. I was out of practice in party-going, so I thought I could get some practice and went to the party even though it was not my favorite activity. I thought I did pretty well for someone out of practice. I spoke to others, remembered names, smiled a lot, and did not stay late. The next day Glenn Perry called me and asked if I would go out with him since he was afraid of me. That was a surprise! I thought I had broken some social rules. I was emerging from the world of teacher / family. I did not know about this other world. I said, "That's an offer I can't refuse." I was like one of the kids in my Special Ed class. How does this work?

Glenn: I went to her house. She took one look at me and said, "How old are you?" I told her, and she said, "Go home. You're a little baby!"

Lee : He came to my house. He looked very young. I asked him how old he was. I was shocked at his age! It was against my beliefs about allowable age differences between women and men. I told him he needed to leave.

Glenn: She was nine years older than me, actually still is, and still with the same incredible being shining in her. "Do you know that's just a program?"

Lee: "What is that?"

Glenn: "Let's go to dinner and I'll tell you."

Lee: We went to dinner at the newly opened Los Angeles area Thai restaurant in Los Feliz. The tastes were brand new. Different. Unfamiliar. Sensations in my shoulders as well as my belly. There was so much to say about it that conversation flowed easily. Then Glenn began to talk about programming. My ears were wide open. The way he described it was so simple and obvious, there was nothing difficult to understand.

This was the picture he drew: If a man is spending "romantic" time with a woman, he must be older than her. Humans make rules about things like that and believe the rules. We choose them. We decide on them. We believe in things and base our thoughts and actions on what we believe. Bright lights were going off in my head. He was letting me in on one of the secrets of the universe. My world was being rearranged. We were in a very large conversation that is ongoing.

Glenn: When I started to see Lee, I started to share my appreciation of the wonderful tool of LSD (common name acid) with her. About a month after starting to see her, I received a call early one Sunday morning. Lee had taken acid the night before, wanted to see me, and asked me to come pick her up at a friend's house. I was disappointed she had done it the first time without me.

She had not had a good time and wanted to see me to get help processing what had happened. I listened and heard everything she said about her experience. I had never mentioned things like set, setting and dosage because she had not mentioned she was interested in doing it. Now she was very interested in the details. She could see that understanding the process could have made all the difference. She probably would not have had difficulty. We had become very trusting of each other. Our conversations were amazing poking grounds of previously called private ideas. It was fun and expansive and led to us living together.

She was willing to try LSD again under my guidance. I was always very excited about introducing new people to what I saw as magic, and I seemed able to pass that on. We wrapped the windows at one corner of the house in black opaque plastic and ingested the acid so we would have no distractions, much like inside the tank, and we could focus fully on what we were doing.

Lee: We were exploring a new world. These were all things I was learning about. I was understanding words and ideas my children talked about and it was most interesting! Here was this new, never before manifest tool (floating) that might save the life of the species on Planet Earth. I was under the magical spell of this remarkably interesting project, and I liked Glenn Perry very much. It was exciting, daring, expanding! Together we were onto something very cool! And for me it was all brand new.

Glenn: Our first date was on July 10, 1974. We decided to be together all of the time less than a month later on Aug 4th.

On July 10, 1975 I went to get my body Rolfed. I came home and told Lee we were going out but would not tell her where. I grabbed a brown paper bag hidden in the back of the refrigerator. We drove to UCLA and parked near their beautiful sculpture garden. As we strolled around the garden I found the correct park bench and asked her to sit. I remained standing. Behind her a woman with a violin moved closer and started playing Mozart's Eine Kleine Nachtmusik. I opened the brown paper bag and showered her with a dozen gardenias, knelt on my right knee, and asked her if she would marry me. She said, "What? Are you serious?" Then she said, "Yes!" I stood and offered my hand for her to stand. We kissed. I suggested we go eat lunch. She agreed. Lee never liked jewelry and I never had any interest in rings so we have never had any. We did have a ring at our wedding.

A close friend of ours, Peter Lit, who I met at a John Lilly workshop a couple of years earlier, contacted us in the middle of June 1976 and asked if we were going to get married: he had a license. We said, "Yes." We contacted a woman friend of ours and together the three of us designed a pair of outfits for the us. July 10, 1976 fortunately fell on a Saturday. I don't like to have to remember too many things so we now had all three anniversaries on the same date. A couple of days before, we had placed sixty-nine yellow and white potted mums around our yard. Two hours before the

Walking down the alsle

wedding Peter, Lee, and I each took a small dose of LSD. A cellist and violinist, who were friends, played chamber music at the edge of the yard while people were being seated. We walked out to an altar and said the vows we had written together. When Peter asked for the ring, the best man rang some Tibetan bells. Lee's son and friends played music. We have been helping each other get enlightened ever since by having a business together while being nearly impossible to get along with, allowing each to learn to keep our equanimity.

Three faces of Lee

CHAPTER FIVE

EXPLORING CONSCIOUSNESS

LSD AS CHANGE AGENT

Glenn, Lee, John Lilly and Rosie

Lee on acid

Glenn

Prior to meeting John Lilly, I had heard stories about LSD as a change agent. In 1967 I attended a show at the Santa Monica Civic Auditorium with Timothy Leary and the Grateful Dead. Leary talked about the League for Spiritual Discovery, a new concept of religion where people with shared spiritual goals came together to expand consciousness. I became interested in LSD to see how it could help my life. By the time I decided I wanted to try it, the establishment had made their decision that anything that opened people's thinking to new possibilities had to be dangerous so it was made illegal, and there were stories that it damaged chromosomes. This had its desired effect on me, it scared me.

At the first John Lilly workshop I attended, he said LSD is not physically dangerous. As they say, a person needs to be especially careful of set, setting and dosage. Set is your mindset, or approach to it; setting is your environment; and dosage is, of course, how much you take. After the workshop I formulated my point of view. My approach was, like anything powerful, it needed to be handled with great care. I never considered it to be something for recreational purposes. For me it was a tool to be used with reverence for the purpose of expanding my consciousness.

After several acid trips, I developed a structure of dosage. I found out that, for me, it would take an hour to start feeling the influence of twenty-five micrograms on an empty stomach. That amount, up to about 250 mics (micrograms), I called an "easy" dose. It might be disorienting for a while but, depending upon how much I took, between thirty and sixty minutes after I felt some sensations, I could still function. I called it a "cosmic" dose if I took 350 mics or more. At that dose, my identity and the universe I was familiar with would dissolve and I would be in new territory. The best way to describe this is I was in a Spiritual place. I would see the energy behind things. I would see more than the consensus reality we all see and share all of the time.

I was always careful to obtain LSD from sources that were safe. Just the same, I quickly developed a procedure to determine the potency of what I received. It was often supplied on perforated blotter paper such that one unit (a tab) was a quarter inch square. I

43

would divide the tab into eight equal parts and take one part every fifteen minutes. Since it took an hour to start feeling the influence of twenty-five mics, when I felt something, I would add up how many parts I had already taken prior to the last sixty minutes, and I would know that amount was twenty-five mics, plus or minus a small error. It was seldom stronger but sometimes lighter than expected. This allowed me to be confident of dosage.

Every time before I took a dose, I would be sure to float every day for one week. When we have been in a mental/emotional funk prior to taking LSD then after taking LSD that is where we end up. If we cannot process that, then we have a negative trip, a bummer. I always made sure to have been in a positive emotional state for a week before taking a cosmic dose or a large easy dose. This handled the mindset.

The first time I dropped I took a medium-sized easy dose. The wife of a couple I was friends with was my guide, and I did it in their home. The memorable incident from that trip was that I visualized a wall with rods sticking out of it. Each rod represented a situation. The farther out of the wall the rod was indicated how positive the situation reflected by that rod was. Whenever one rod went in, another one or more had to come out an equal amount to balance the energy. It showed me how everything in the universe is in balance. The other thing memorable was listening to a Vivaldi guitar piece. On side B was Mauro Giuliani's "First Guitar Concerto, Op 30" played by John Williams. It became one of my three favorite pieces of music.

On another trip, after I met Lee, I asked her whether she remembered me playing that Giuliani piece. She said "No," paused and then said, "Oh, I do remember seeing it." "What do you mean?" She drew a picture of what she saw, which was basically dancing colored crystals. I indicated that is what I saw when I heard him on acid. She later made a painting of it on a cloth. When a woman we had tripped with saw it, she said, "Oh, Giuliani!"

My first cosmic dose I did in my apartment. The guide was a good friend I had met at my first workshop with John Lilly. I was lying on my mattress on the floor, and he was sitting on cushions in the lotus position nearby, facing me. When I started to feel the effect, the sensations became very intense very quickly. I was nauseous, tingly all over, and everything looked like it was under water. I became terrified that I had done something I should not have done—but it was too late to back out now. I had no idea what to do. I looked at my friend, and he was there calmly sitting in the lotus position. That calmed me down. That momentary experience was particularly important to me. It reminded me of the importance of having a guide. In addition, I understood that if someone was having an intense experience you can be the guide for them by simply being calm and present, without any agenda.

I had quite a few LSD experiences prior to getting together with Lee. I was starting to see that the universe was far more expansive and interesting than I had previously imagined. It became a place of magic. Before, the universe was full of objects and physical things; now it was also filled with energy. Plants and animals became more alive. My heart was opening. I was no longer living only in my head. When Lee had her first trip she did not have the information about set, setting and dosage. After reading this Lee said, "I wish I would have had this information when I had my first acid trip. It could have eliminated some of the discomfort I experienced."

A couple of years after becoming involved with Lee my father developed prostate cancer. I was home with him for a week and wondered why he did not seem to be making use of the last part of his life. Three months later, my mother called to say he now had pneumonia. Was I flying home to see him? I said yes, so she said she would start giving him antibiotics until she was sure I would get there in time and then would stop. She and he both felt it was time for him to go so that was a good way to do it. I arrived and not too much later, he passed. I thought I had handled my grief, but three weeks later, I was feeling out of sorts and I could not understand what was going on. I dropped a large dose of acid to find out. I was lying on our bed and Lee was sitting with me. Early in the trip she put on Durufle's Requiem, another one of my three favorite pieces of music, which I often would play during a trip.

I immediately became my father during that last period of his life. I started to process the unresolved issues in my life. I handled them one at a time until they were settled, and I was now ready to leave this world. Lee saw me turn into my father and, when I was ready to leave, she became worried I was going to split. I knew at some level that I was not my father, so I returned to myself. I saw that my father had spent his last days processing everything he needed so he could leave. Do we all have to complete certain things before we die? I, myself, am doing everything I can to complete processing as many unresolved emotional issues as possible now so I do not have to hang out for years taking care of old business.

Not all our experiences were at home. A friend told us of a mine shaft that went horizontally into a mountain in the Mojave Desert. We thought it would be great to trip in the earth. We entered the shaft in the morning and went in far enough that, with our flashlight off, we could not see the light of the mine entrance. We took a very large "easy" dose of acid and agreed to have the lights off and not talk during the trip, until we changed our minds. After several hours I thought I would like us to speak. Lee thought, that's fine. I was confused. I thought, if that's fine how come she didn't say it. She then said out loud, "That's fine." In comparing notes, we both agreed that during the trip we communicated more completely during those hours telepathically than we ever had with each other or anyone else in any way before. I continued to have that feeling of being continually present for close to a week.

Lee

We were in Northern California in Redwood City and John had two dolphins he was studying there. I was invited to swim with them. I quickly became fearful that I could not deal with them swimming under the water. Telepathically hearing my thoughts, they immediately stopped going under the water and swam around on top. Then we started throwing a volleyball back and forth and they made sure to include everyone there.

Glenn

After doing LSD many times I had three trips that were quite different. They were cosmic doses, and halfway through the trips I found myself in an extremely unpleasant universe, that I thought would last forever, where I did not understand the rules nor how to function. I do not remember a lot about those trips, but I do remember something about one of them. I started trying to work my way out of the predicament I was in. I started thinking that I was "one" and there was "not me," and that made "two." I continued trying to use logic to work my way out, but I do not remember more details. Each time, eventually the acid wore off and I came back to the universe I had left. Several months later I realized I was having problems with my blood sugar during that period. I thought I was going crazy and might need to be institutionalized. Eventually, I found out I was hypoglycemic. On occasion Lee and I would be driving home, and I would suddenly feel intense rage. When we got home I would eat something, and I would go back to normal almost instantly. I came to understand that I was having a hypoglycemia attack during these three acid trips where I was not eating anything for several hours. It was reassuring to know that I could survive something that intense. A year or two later, I recovered from this hypoglycemic condition. I have done acid sessions since then but not too many. This was a lot to process.

I tried LSD once in the tank and immediately fear of suffocation appeared. I climbed out and did not try it again. I have always felt more interested in taking it with someone, and Lee has always been the perfect partner for that, so I never had the urge to deal with the suffocation fear. I would encourage anyone doing LSD to have a guide along rather than doing it solo. Also, I would suggest not including too many variables in a trip. As I think about it, I strongly discourage anyone from using the tank as a place for experimenting with strong drugs of any sort. Remember to float only when you are comfortable.

I credit acid with opening my heart faster than I otherwise would have. I feel blessed to have been able to do it.

John's Research Into Consciousness

John has been criticized for being a drug addict during a period of taking Ketamine several times a day for a number of months. We were around him a lot during this period. What we saw was this: a researcher of consciousness doing what they did their whole life. If he spent his whole life researching consciousness, how did he do that? How does anyone research consciousness? First the research must be performed on oneself. The person needs to observe their mind, their thoughts and their habits. It is necessary for them to notice when they are conscious and when they are doing things automatically. You can get a clear picture of what this is like by sitting still and observing. Do this for half an hour twice a day for six months, and you will have a tiny bit of appreciation for what John was doing much of his life.

He ran lots of experiments to determine what influenced one's consciousness. For example, He took canned tuna, put it in the microwave and ate it for a week, and did it again without using the microwave. From the simple to the sublime, he was constantly investigating what affected consciousness.

We often visited with Sasha and Ann Shulgin, authors of *Pihkal: A Chemical Love Story*, during the period that John was taking Ketamine. Hearing concerns by some around John, we asked Sasha if we needed to worry about him. Sasha, together with his wife Ann and a group of close friends, researched close to two hundred substances that he thought might have positive mind-altering effects, like LSD and mescaline. He laughed and said we did not need to worry about John. If Sasha, referred to by some as the godfather of psychedelics, was not worried, we surely did not need to worry. After all, John had access to legal LSD through his colleagues at the National Institutes and declined their offers during his first ten years of isolation tank research, the time he needed to develop his own personal baseline. To maintain the purity of his research, it was his practice to keep variables to a minimum. Once he had thoroughly explored a domain he would extend his research by adding a new variable.

John sometimes gave us exceptional help from unusual domains. He related to me a story that can be found in his *Simulations of God: The Science of Belief.* In a research study he inserted electrodes into monkey's brains and discovered that the processes of sexual arousal, erection, ejaculation and orgasm are not tied to each other. There are separate subroutines for each of these phenomena, found in different areas of the brain, independent of each other. Sometime later, Lee and I did a cosmic dose of LSD and although it was difficult, I managed to turn on our stereo system to play one of Mozart's violin concertos. We started making love. Within five minutes we both started orgasming and both continued until the concerto ended at which time we stopped what we were doing.

A short time later, I was able to put on Beethoven's Third Piano Concerto. We lay on our backs and listened to the music, the last of my three favorite pieces of music, which we also occasionally played while tripping. We both immediately became points of consciousness as we drifted up into clear crystalline light. What we experienced made our previous experience pale in comparison to what we now felt. The feeling cannot be put into words.

Another time we had the experience of becoming one. After hanging out as a single entity, the merged entity became bored. It wanted someone to play with. To become playmates we had to re-create differences. Then we were two.

We will share that each float is perfect for the floater at the time of the float even if it seems negative or insignificant. This reminds me of Milton Erickson, a psychiatrist who specialized in medical hypnosis and family therapy. At the age of seventeen he contracted polio so debilitating it resulted in very limited mobility. Unable to move, he took the opportunity to study communication, observing the ten other members of his family in their interactions. He was also color blind and tone deaf. He attributed his extraordinary capacity to focus on aspects of communication that were usually overlooked, to his "liabilities." Through emphasizing the positive, he was often able to achieve cures within very few sessions that others had failed to accomplish over many years. He saw that his exceptional abilities were the result of what others considered his "handicaps." He never saw anyone's problems as negative but as assets, and he would use people's problems as tools in the service of helping them transcend their situation. One of his techniques was to use hypnosis to activate the unconscious mind to assist creativity and problem solving.

He treated a teenager with a serious fingernail biting problem. He suggested that she was missing out on something. She obviously enjoyed biting her nails a great deal so she should save one of her nails for two or three weeks without biting it so she could have a whole nail to savor. By giving her the job of abstaining from biting one nail, she was developing the habit and ability to refrain from nail biting. After that success she could expand her learned ability.

His example taught me to look to my own experience to reveal reality, and not be concerned about other people's definitions. The purpose of this story is to recommend that we do not go after John Lilly's or anyone's experiences in the tank or with LSD but trust our own experiences will be perfect for us.

Lee's picture of Glenn on acid

CHAPTER SIX:
CONSCIOUSNESS AND FLOATING
WHO IS IN CONTROL?

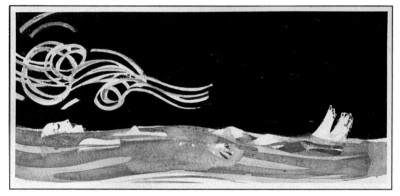

Andy Rush - Watercolor

Look Mom, I'm walking!

Glenn

Imagine yourself as a toddler, only one year old. You are learning to walk, struggling with your very first steps. Picture yourself in your dining room. You crawl over to the chair with the ladder back so you can use it to pull yourself up to standing. It takes some time, but you succeed. (After all, you have done this several times before.) Firmly holding onto the middle bar, you carefully pull yourself up until you are sure you are balanced on both legs. It is an achievement, and you are thrilled by it.

Now you feel ready to try something new. You push with your right leg to put your weight solely on your left foot. Hesitantly, you rotate to the right, letting go of the chair with one hand, still holding on with the other. You lift your right leg and move it forward and down. You start to transfer your weight onto your right leg and you lose your balance. You fall to the floor, laughing.

You crawl over to the chair to try again.

This kind of focused attention and experimentation allows you to learn very quickly to walk. You use similar attention and presence to learn to eat and talk and all the other things babies and young children learn in the first few years of life. When learning any of these skills, you are fully present with great attention. You are constantly watching the people around you and trying experiments to see what works and what does not. During this period of our lives we are generally present; we are generally conscious and aware.

As adults, when we walk or talk or eat, the experiences when we were young are used by the brain to allow us to do these activities without our conscious participation. We can walk down a crowded city street while talking with a friend without focusing any of our attention on our walking or how to talk. These activities are handled totally automatically by our brains. Most adult activities are done this way. Besides walking and talking, once we learn to drive, cook, and even argue, these are mostly done automatically. We can focus on the content of an argument rather than how to do one. How to do one is automatic, in other words, done by a particular part of the brain, using past experiences.

Dr. Marcus E. Raichle, a neurologist, in 2001 discovered a part of the brain now called the Default Mode Network (DMN). One of the functions of this network is to track sensory input and find experiences from the past that relate to the situation at hand. As soon as it finds the relevant information, it ignores further input and gives the brain the earlier experiences to use in handling the current situation. That is, it limits the amount of input we receive to an absolute minimum, just enough to know what past experiences to access.

This is extremely useful. When a tiger is headed toward us, jaws open and salivating, we do not need to think about what to do. Instead the brain tells us, based on previous experiences, whether we should run or pray. It is important for us as adults to be efficient. This only happens with situations involving activities about which we have prior experience. The time for learning and experimentation is childhood. Adulthood is for using the experiences from when we were young to function efficiently and automatically. I want to prepare omelets for the guests that have arrived and are sitting at the pass-through in front of the stove where I am going to cook them—the omelets, not the guests. I have done all these things many times before. My brain pulls up routines from the past, as easily and automatically as walking, with little conscious participation. While I am cooking, I can put my focus on talking to my guests.

This local big cat didn't head towards us with open jaws.
Photo credit: Wayne Hoyle

Dr. Robin Carhart-Harris, a neuroscientist researching the working of people's brains when they are on psychedelics, found the DMN is not active when they are on psychedelics or have been meditating. At these times, we are incredibly open. Without the intrusion of earlier experiences, we get a much wider range of input and possibilities in the present. That is where babies and young children spend their time. It turns out that they are better at solving problems that require thinking outside the box. Let me repeat that.

Young children are better at solving problems that require thinking outside the box. This is because they are not being fed data from the past that keeps them from receiving all the sensory input. Dr. Alison Gopnik, a child psychology professor and associate professor of philosophy at UC Berkeley, created a music box experiment where the music would only start when the proper colored block was set on it. Halfway through the experiment she changed the setting so that it required two blocks to work. In testing four-year-old children and college students, the four-year-olds did significantly better than the college students. The children were far more willing to consider and try possibilities outside the box. Their job as young children is to explore all possibilities. They are excellent at trying anything. Not such a good procedure to follow when a tiger is headed our way.

Dr. Gopnik is struck by the similarities between the LSD experience and her understanding of the consciousness of children. For example: seeing more possibilities, diffused attention, magical thinking, and less sense of self. She suggests, "If you want to understand what an expanded consciousness looks like, all you have to do is have tea with a four-year-old." She says, "The child's brain is extremely plastic,

Expanding our consciousness with Sophia
Photo credit: Laylah Hali

good for learning, not accomplishing," better for "exploring rather than exploiting." It has a great many more neural connections than the adult brain. Once we are adults, the neural connections we have used the most remain and unused ones disappear.

As adults, our past experiences are used to solve current problems. We only come up with solutions that our past experiences point to. That is why we cannot think outside the box. We only use whatever our experiences dictate. Einstein said, "No problem can be solved by the same kind of thinking that created it." Lots of our problems need a different kind of thinking. How do you turn off the DMN so you can consider all possibilities and think outside the box?

As previously mentioned, a four-year-old could help us, or we could take psychedelics since the DMN does not work during an acid session or after we have been meditating or floating frequently, or for long enough. So, we could meditate or float. A lot of meditators think that floating is the ultimate place to meditate. They find it makes meditating much easier and more effective. That has certainly been my experience. I think floating is the ultimate place to be creative because it allows us to move into a conscious state where the DMN is not active. Anytime I have a highly creative job to do, I float a lot, at least every day. Actually, I generally float every day anyway. As a result, I have become far more creative outside the tank than I used to be inside.

The DMN chooses what it uses to solve current problems. For example, as an adult Lee started public speaking and found it terrifying. She floated and kept her focus on the fear, simply experiencing it. It took several times floating before she found the following.

Lee

I was about five years old and my tap dance class was performing on a wooden floor. We were excited! It must have been a springtime special show of what we were learning. Ten of us were dressed in costumes, standing in a line facing the audience in the school gym. The audience was out there, sitting on folding chairs, mainly our parents. I was wearing a silvery top, short black pants, black shoes with a small heel and big taps on the toes. We had been tapping three or four minutes. It was fun.

Suddenly, I could feel my pants creeping then sliding down my legs. I felt nervous and anxious. Scared! And I did not know what to do. I felt my pants moving down. The audience started laughing very loud and pointing at us; pointing to where I was dancing. And

I did not know what to do. I knew my pants fell down. I picked my pants up and kept dancing. Embarrassed! I felt just terrible that I messed up.

Then and there I made a decision: I cannot go on stage. I cannot do that.

The brain never asks us for our rating or ranking of experiences when they are stored, whether they should be used, valued or thrown out. It stores them all. The brain also does not ask us whether we agree with the experiences chosen now to solve the current problem. It figures out on its own how to value them and what to use for any situation.

As an adult, if I think about performing, my pants drop. I really mean I get nervous. I floated and eventually discovered this incident and the decision I had made. I released that decision and made a new one.

Glenn

To have a high quality of life we cannot let the brain always arbitrarily choose its selection from the past to handle a problem in the present.

The automatic functioning of the DMN is not always choosing the preferred past experiences. To change that, we have to work hard to become conscious and not allow the unconscious functioning of our brain to control our life for us.

Besides floating, John Lilly gave us the gift of inspiring us to include expanding our consciousness as a high priority in our life. John said, "It is my firm belief that experiencing higher states of consciousness is necessary for the survival of the human species." We invite you also to make expanding your consciousness a high priority in your life by floating or meditating more.

CHAPTER SEVEN

CREATING A LIFE OF INTENTION

SAMADHI TANK DESIGN, MANUFACTURE, AND FIRST FLOATERS

Lee and Glenn in Wedding Outfits

Cardboard tank with supports, no frame

Glenn

As soon as we decided to go full time with the tank company, I quit my job at SDS, which had been sold to Xerox five years before. They closed that division a year after I quit. Lee quit teaching at the end of that school year.

The original tank was designed as a rectangular chest-high box with entry through a hatch at one end of the top. To get up and over and down into the tank there was a small ladder. Without another ladder inside, it was almost impossible to get out. To solve that, below the hatch, on the side, above the level of the solution, a door was cut that would swing open. The problem with this vertical side door was that condensation formed that would drip down onto the floor. Unacceptable!

Here was a problem and the only solution created another problem: the condensation falling on the floor. I became so frustrated I began to doubt my decision to quit my day job when I only had an idea, and not even a viable tank design. As I was describing the problem to Lee, it suddenly occurred to me that maybe I was looking in the wrong place. Perhaps the problem I needed to solve was how to enter a chest high box. How many different modes of entry could there be? Why had I not considered any others? I knew about different ways of defining the problem when I was a computer programmer. How had I not thought of that now?

During a morning shower my attention was drawn to the wood shingles on the walls. At about chest height the wall protruded into the space with a forty-five-degree slope at the top. As I looked at that slope, it came to me: I could shorten the front and the top and put the door in that area at a forty-five-degree slant. There might be some condensation rolling down, but it could be controlled. Eureka! Next, I started to work on the exterior shell to hold everything in and keep light out, with affordable insulation to maintain the tank temperature inexpensively. After my experience with the entry door, I started brainstorming in my own mind and with others all the materials I could think of for the structure and the insulation regardless of whether I thought they would work. Cardboard came up. I was determined to be open even though it was a most unlikely solution. I continued to explore because it met many of my other criteria. Thinking it through, I saw the salt solution in a vinyl liner, leaving only the top, door and door structure pieces exposed to the one hundred percent humidity inside the tank. I wondered, since the cardboard was porous, could the moisture go right through the material and not be a problem. Would Styrofoam sheets be a good inexpensive solution for insulation? I assumed so.

In my investigation of cardboard I discovered tri-wall which has three layers of corrugation and is more than four times as thick as regular single-ply cardboard. This makes it strong enough to be used for the shipping carton. The idea was for the shipping carton to be a five-sided tray, in other words a box with an open top, made from tri-wall. The top could be another five-sided box with the opening facing down, out of regular single-ply. Thinking outside the box brought me right into the box.

The box could withstand the stresses of shipping. Upon receipt, the customer could remove everything and nest the bottom inside the shipping top. Next the back, front and sides of the cardboard and Styrofoam could be placed vertically in the tri-wall shipping carton/ tank bottom nested in the carton top, resulting in nothing for the landfill. The vinyl liner could be set in, and the top and door and door structure put on. They would have a very inexpensive, lightweight, ecologically sensitive (no shipping material waste) tank, a persistent design criteria focus throughout our history.

I got the materials and made a prototype. I added a waterbed heater under the liner, plugged into a temperature control. Experimentation showed I needed to put a wood frame at the top of the carton/ tank bottom to prevent the sides from bowing out. I researched an inexpensive pump and filter. To have a supply of fresh air I added a fan in a cardboard box connected to the

Cardboard Tank Packed Up

tank with a black opaque hose. I was able to fit all these things into a cavity in the shipping carton, and Lee and I could carry the whole carton containing the complete unassembled tank ourselves.

This sounds very straightforward, but it took about three months for me to work it all out. I found a Styrofoam supplier to create the door and door structure with tongue and grooves to keep the parts together. I got three sets from him, and we started painting black epoxy onto the Styrofoam door and structure to keep light out. It took twenty-four hours to paint one set, and the results were shockingly poor. After three sets, it became obvious that we needed another solution. After working on it for three weeks, I was pulling my hair out. Though I was only thirty-four years old, I had started losing my hair long before. When I was twenty-six I went scuba diving in Mexico at Isla Tiburon (Shark Island). Now that was a story. Just kidding, nothing happened, I mean with sharks. Shark attacks are exceedingly rare. Most varieties of sharks have no interest in eating people. None. When we came back home, and we got the photos from our trip developed, I looked at them and in one I was facing away from the camera. It was hard to believe. I was mostly bald on the back of my head. I had no idea. Eight years later there was not a lot of hair left to pull.

Back to the Tanks

What should we do? Lee suggested we talk to the Styrofoam supplier. It had always been her idea to get problems solved by talking to people. Not being a people person, that rarely entered my mind. He suggested using vacuum formed plastic sheets for the door and its structure.

We contacted three vacuum-forming companies. Two of them were not pleasant experiences; they were not helpful or interested in the project. The third, Don, was a match. Not only did he want our business, he was interested in our product. Don made the molds to our specifications and formed two plastic door and structure samples. We used the existing Styrofoam with these new plastic parts. It worked beautifully. We finally had a tank we could use and sell. Now, where to put ours? We selected a corner of our home office with the proper dimensions, unfortunately full of stuff.

VACUUM FORMING

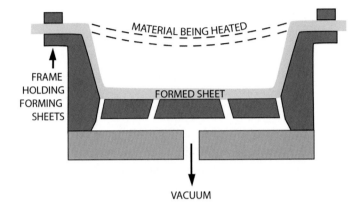

HEATER

MATERIAL BEING HEATED

FRAME HOLDING FORMING SHEETS

FORMED SHEET

VACUUM

WHEN SHEET IS HEATED IT SAGS AND THE VACUUM IS TURNED ON.
THE PART IS COOLED, THEN REMOVED AND TRIMMED.

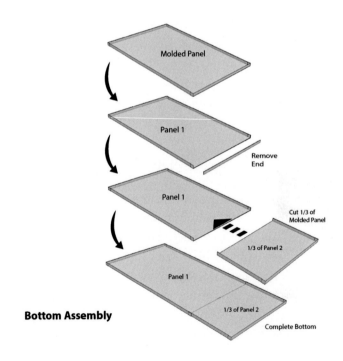

Molded Panel

Panel 1

Remove
End

Panel 1

Cut 1/3 of
Molded Panel

1/3 of Panel 2

Panel 1

Bottom Assembly

1/3 of Panel 2

Complete Bottom

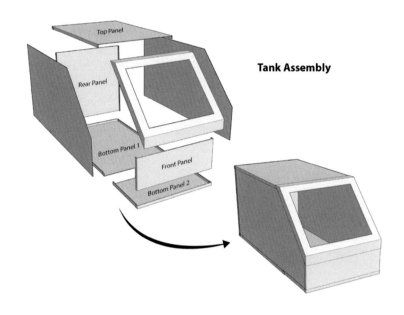

Drawings from Jim Rodney showing vacuum forming.

Finished Model

We built a raised structure to hold the material and placed the tank underneath, filled it with solution and immediately began floating.

Lee

Now we needed to make some tanks to sell. We did not have a way to make them at home, and we did not have a factory. The cardboard company would cut and bend each piece but because of the setup fee we needed to buy many sets. Here we were, working from our house. If we had materials for fifty tanks, we would not even have enough room for storage, never mind assembly.

We were in sunny Southern California. At that time you could be certain that it would not rain in the summer so we thought to store the finished tanks outside. We had a big front yard, and we planned to stack them on skids, eight high, and ship as needed. We could cover the tanks with tarps when it began to rain in the winter.

We asked our Styrofoam supplier, with whom we had developed a close relationship, if we could use his space. We got a lesson in insurance and liability. The liability of having us work inside his factory was too risky. However, outside was a different matter. He had a long, narrow area between his building and the building next door, about twenty feet wide by two hundred feet long. It was fenced and he lent us that outside space for one weekend. We set up a game called "Assembly Line." We invited thirteen of our friends to come and play for the weekend. This was in September when it was still light enough to work outside until about 8:00 P.M.

Glenn and I spent a few weeks getting ready for the game. We prepared all the subassemblies necessary to keep the line moving: all the fan boxes, bagged clamps, prepared packages of diatomaceous earth, and all the other necessary components. In addition we put together the doors and door structures, we made the wooden frames to support the tank walls, and we made many of the tools required including a big flat cart on wheels to move the tank carton along the assembly line.

We organized the materials so that folding and taping the tri-wall base of the tank was the first operation. That was a two-person job. The tri-wall was very heavy, and although scored, took a lot of pressure to bend. We folded it at the score and held it together with strong packing tape. Since this tape was on the outside and could be seen, the taping needed to be done carefully. The tri-wall base was loaded onto the cart and rolled to the next station. Next, the foam bottom was inserted followed by a custom-made plastic liner to hold the solution. The next two people laid the Styrofoam and cardboard sides down into the carton over the liner. The carton moved down the line with the remaining pieces being added. At the last station were strapping tools. The completed tank box was strapped closed and loaded onto a truck.

The game took a while to learn. We all realized very quickly that, if we made a mistake, someone somewhere in the world was going to have a problem when they received their new Samadhi Tank. We did not want to pass problems on to new tank owners. We worked slowly and carefully until we felt sure of the moves. Glenn and I ran back and forth to each station making sure that our friends knew what they were doing. When it got dark, we had fifteen tanks loaded onto the truck. We then drove across town to our house. Some people unloaded the tanks, some helped to prepare food, and some rested. We had a good evening of eating, telling stories of the day, and making music.

The next morning, we met again at the factory parking lot. We still had thirty-five tanks to complete, more than double what we had managed to complete the previous day. Before noon the most unusual happened; the sky clouded over, threatening rain. Sure enough, a few sprinkles came down and it did not look good for us. We scrambled to find ways to cover the cardboard as our large stack of materials would not survive a downpour. We stood inside the factory watching and waiting. It lasted about an hour. Everyone was worried. We did not consider failure as a possibility. We were sure we could succeed and when the rain stopped, as quickly as it had started, we danced back out to work.

We loaded the fiftieth tank onto the truck as darkness was setting in, cleaned up and headed for our celebration at home. We were exuberant! How could work be so much fun? We all felt so good it made us think people would want to pay to be a part of working this way! This was the kind of magic that seemed to be part of being around the tanks, and around John Lilly!

Being the only ones working with floatation tanks at the time, our attention at the very beginning was mainly on the design. Immediately after that we turned our attention towards how to introduce people to their use. In the beginning, when people asked us what we did we would say: "We make isolation tanks. They are eight feet long, four feet wide and four feet high containing ten inches of water with seven hundred pounds of Epsom salt dissolved in it. They are light proof and soundproof. You get in, lie face up in the solution and float. It is dark and wet, and you go in all by yourself" and so on. People would say, "Why would you want to do that?" We just laughed. People we talked to were definitely not interested, and so we spent all the time we were in the car together trying to come up with the words that we could use that would not turn people off when we described what we were doing.

Once we developed it fully, we said, "We make floatation tanks. They are a little bit larger around than a twin bed, chest high. There are ten inches of water to which so much Epsom salt has been added that when you get in and lie face up, you float like a cork, weightless like an astronaut in space. It is enclosed with a lightweight door you can leave open, or if you want to get rid of the distractions of noise and light you can close it."

Many of the first people who came to float had studied John Lilly's work. He had a big following and the ones who worked with him the most were the most eager to repeat as many floats as they were able to fit in their life. We were eager to have as large a research sample as we could fit into our available time, and we allowed people to float as many times as we could fit them in. We were so certain what we were not to do, and so uncertain about getting it right that we made time before and after each float to be with each person for our research into various ways of supporting their experience. The several hundred people who came and used the tank allowed us to learn how to introduce and how to end a float.

Glenn

Lee has a naturally welcoming attitude. She had a special way of greeting first time floaters, friendly and curious, answering questions, providing clear information about procedures and housekeeping, with no programming, to clear the path for them to have their own unique experience. Before every float Lee would carefully describe how to exit the tank: stand up in the tank doorway before getting out and squeegee the solution from your body; then raise a leg and dry it off before stepping out; then bring out the other leg and wipe it off before putting your foot down into the towel lined tray. The last step is to dry your hair until it is drip-free. Then, walk lightly to the bathroom shower. We did this for four years to prevent salt solution being tracked everywhere. This was the motivation to subsequently design the commercial tank and shower into a single unit.

I created a simple protocol for tank solution maintenance. We used our filtration system and chlorine bleach for twenty-five minutes after each floater to be sure everything was clean for the next. After the person floated and showered, they would come out to the main room. Lee would usually talk to them. One of her methods was to repeat the question asked to be sure she heard it correctly, for herself and for the person asking. The repetition demonstrated that they were both together in the conversation. I would be in the same area usually working on design or finances.

After the floater left, Lee and I often discussed their conversation. I would ask her questions about why she acted or spoke the way she did. She would explain so I could understand her approach. I was learning from her how to be with people, without an agenda. As we learned we began to role play: well, gee, you could have said this or you could have changed your tune that way to something else. Exploring what she did made it more conscious for both of us.

One of the most surprising things was how many of the people who came to float spoke about positive changes to their health: quitting smoking was big and changing diet was very big. They were consuming more vegetables and less sugar; saying how much better they felt when they switched to "good" food. They were exercising more and they looked better. The mid 70s was not a time that health was talked about as much as it is now in 2020.

It was also surprising that many of the floaters spoke freely about old upsetting issues they cleared while or after floating. They were open about these things, as it seemed concerns about privacy had fallen away. They were also willing to be very simply quiet. No need to look or sound as if there was something they were supposed to be doing or being. Very nice to be around them.

Lee's way was very unusual. Lee was a people person, actually still is. People persons normally enjoy talking more than listening. Much later I learned part of the history of her skill. She had a lisp as a child. Being strongly discouraged from talking with a lisp, she simply gave up talking. She developed the highly unusual attribute of totally listening to another, without needing to comment, give advice, offer help, make small talk or do any of the myriad other things people do when they make conversation. I am someone who sees the structure of things. My interest in structure and Lee's people skills gave us the tools to take what was happening and formulate it into something that we could, much later, teach our staff when we opened our float center. We developed our entire approach right there, with the hundred first floaters teaching us what worked to support their experience.

I was an excellent designer. Lee was excellent at listening to others. I designed a tank. Lee worked on introducing people to it. We worked together, clear about our direction. It allowed us to always know where we were going! A couple of floaters asked about having their own tank. With fifty tanks in our front yard, we needed to do something. We started exploring the process of sales: how it worked, what the objective was and how to do it without undermining the sanctity of the floating experience we had established for the floater. This last was especially important, requiring great delicacy and went along with our distaste for pressure selling.

Since we were at the early stages of developing our business, we would encounter issues like how to sell. Then we would start to explore. I would find something we were in the dark about that we needed to learn, and ask questions. Lee would propose an answer, and we would pull it apart, dissect it, discuss it, each adding something or asking another question. Once that was explored, and we were clear, we would ask another question. It was exciting to be discovering new universes and learning new abilities. We were taking something that was fuzzy and confusing, and bringing light and clarity to it. We would then try what we had figured out and adjust it based on input from the real world.

Production in factory of plastic tank

With sales we did a lot of role-playing, usually switching sides so we could each feel how the customer felt as well as how we felt as the salesperson. We came up with the idea that our job as salespeople was to become clear. We needed first to be clear about what the person wanted. We used the listen and repeat technique, demonstrating that we were together in the conversation. To discover if it was appropriate to help them, and if so, how, it was important to discover the details of their situation. In all of this we had to be like the tank: empty. We were not to be invested in any agenda. If we were attached to an outcome, it might be felt as pressure and the whole situation could become negative. If we had no needs, and no energy on a particular result, they would not mind anything we asked. Sales became lots of fun.

Developing the Deluxe

The tank business was picking up and we were looking for a commercial alternative. Our customers were asking for a "nicer" tank; not cardboard, and washable to remove the salt solution. (Frank Gehry's elevation of cardboard to art furniture predated our tank by three years but not everyone was paying attention.) In response, we decided to replace the cardboard with the same plastic sheet material the door and door structure were made of.

I wanted to thermoform the top, back, front and bottom. Don, the thermoformer, was limited to making parts only as long as the length of the top, which was significantly shorter than the bottom. But after considerable thinking and some floats, the idea came to make a single mold the size of the top. By forming it four times we could make all the necessary pieces: one for the top, one for the back and front, and one and a third for the bottom. A satisfyingly elegant and economical solution ended up requiring only one small inexpensive mold to make the four pieces. (Editor: See drawings on bottom of pg 64 and top of 65)

To strengthen the thin plastic sheets to make them usable, we decided to adhere them to the Styrofoam insulation. Since we did not have a factory, and the basement was far too small, I started using the living room to test the production methods. At this point we were more than ready to move production into a factory, which we were able to find soon thereafter. Now we needed jigs, templates and tools for unique-to-us processes. During my morning float I would think through possible designs needed for our manufacturing process, building them in my mind. When I found a problem in my design, I would rework it and rebuild it until it was solved. I would go to the factory and, having made and corrected my mistakes while floating, the construction would go quickly. My floats were significant time-savers.

After completing the design of the commercial tank and beginning production we brought one in to be certified for the first time by the City of Los Angeles Building and Safety Electrical Testing Laboratory. We were very pleasantly surprised; this strange box of ours passed certification without any corrections.

It was important to test out the Samadhi floatation tank and to be able to show it to people. When Lee's daughter, Shoshana, moved out of the family house we set up the new Deluxe tank in her vacated bedroom. Now we had two tanks, each in their own separate rooms, operating in our home. There was just one bathroom with a tub shower. We staggered the float start times so no one would have to wait for their shower, and we could take our time answering questions with people coming for their first float. When a couple came together, one would wait fifteen minutes before beginning their float. The one waiting could sit, read, or we talked together.

When we had completed designing the Samadhi Deluxe, rented a factory, and designed and made tools for producing it, we started work on a brochure: a promotional piece to help with sales. We needed photos and we had a large stock of new four by eight-foot sheets of white Styrofoam insulation waiting to be cut. We attached these to the walls and floor of an empty corner of our newly leased factory. One of the frequent floaters at our home was a photographer for Life magazine, a popular periodical of the time. He thought he could do a good job and was happy to trade for floating. Asking several floaters, we were able to find people who were willing to model with the tank in the nude.

Some years earlier we had had our first experience photographing the tank when a friend had offered to take some tank photos. We borrowed an art gallery, got some friends and family for models, and he took a bunch of photos. We gave him no direction because we did not know how to guide him. When the photos came back from the developer what we saw was a lot of people and, if we looked closely enough, there was a tank hidden somewhere in the background. Unfortunately, the photographer had been focused on people rather than on the tank. He was good with people, but we obviously needed something else; that was a good learning experience. This time we did a lot of groundwork with the photographer. In truth, none of us knew what would work so JP, the photographer, suggested we spend one weekend trying all sorts of things and capturing it on film. We could then review the contact sheets to see what we liked and set up the actual shots for the next weekend. The first weekend went well. This was the hippy era and nudity was not a big deal, especially within our market.

We saw what we liked from the first weekend and saw how to change some of the shots to improve them. The second weekend we took a massive number of black and white photos for the brochure and, with another camera, took a few color shots in case we needed something for the media. When we got the color slides back they

73

looked beautiful. When we looked at the black and white we found that the rental camera had failed and none of the hundreds of photos we took came out. It was so discouraging. To do it again we would need not only the photographer and ourselves but the models as well. We were looking for three good shots. We had something we could use from the first weekend for one but we had nothing for the most important two.

After long deliberation we decided not to spend any more money on this project. We returned to the factory with our own camera and each took photos of the other. Luckily, we had learned enough from the two full weekends of shooting that it took only fifteen minutes. When they were developed we decided they were exactly what we needed. No experience is a failure. They all give valuable lessons we can use the rest of our life. We have had forty-eight years of valuable experiences.

Lee

One Monday afternoon we heard someone coming up the walkway of our house, on almost an acre, set back from the street. On the front corner of the lot was a small house above the garage with a walkway between it and a large redwood. In the front along the property line at the street was a hedge of tall bushes, completely blocking any view of the house from the street. It was warm out and the front door was open. In an overly thick German accent, this booming demanding voice yells, "Is this the Cosmic Coffin Company?"

It had to be a friend. I went to the door, and now we are laughing with Robin Williams in Lederhosen. He had become a friend of John Lilly and talked with him about tanks. He wanted his own and came to Samadhi to get it. He was a clown and looked extremely happy being a clown. We delivered and installed his tank and went to help him with it a few times before he moved to San Francisco. He acted as if he were a member of the family, like many of the people who came to float.

Walkway Up to Echo Park House,
photo credit: Paul Levitt

CHAPTER EIGHT

SO MUCH FEAR
WHAT FIRST TIME FLOATERS
NEED TO KNOW

Questions Questions, E.J. Gold

Clinging To The Content Of The Mind, E.J. Gold

"Let me assert my firm belief that the only
thing we have to fear is...fear itself."

Franklin D. Roosevelt
First inaugural address March 4th, 1933

Anything can happen in the tank—from the rewards of consciousness, deep rest, creative insight, heavenly dreams, confrontation with fears, finding the door to peace, to experiencing the ridiculous. John Lilly used floating to investigate and explore consciousness. What is in the way of being more conscious? Fear!

Lee

After two years of floating every day first thing in the morning, I found myself in the tank with this large fear of the dark, and I felt scared! At first, all my attention went to feeling scared, and I stayed with that fear until I could quiet down, until I could ask myself, "What is going on? Did someone leave something here?" After I was quieted enough to sit up, I opened the door and breathed slowly until I felt comfortable enough to lie down again. I did that three or four times while I was looking for the place that was so scary to me. About the fourth time, I saw myself as a little kid with my two much older sisters playing our game where I was the doll pushed into the dark closet. We played this regularly. It really scared me, and I was obviously still carrying the fear, thirty-five years later.

In our first year of being full-time with Samadhi we noticed that many people had fears before their first float. Ken Russell, the director of the 1980 movie *Altered States*, sheepishly came out of the tank a little more than ten minutes after he went in, saying he had recently been caught in an elevator when the power went off. Toni Lilly (John Lilly's wife), even after she had been floating for a few years, panicked and popped out the top of the tank, prompting John to ask us to make sure floaters could find the door when we gave them the orientation. When panicked, people can behave very unpredictably. It can be assumed the first thing a floater will do is try to get out, fast, spurred by the "fight or flight" reflex. Thinking where the door is is not the first thing most people will do in that situation nor can we expect them to look for a light switch.

During our introduction to the tank we ask that when they first get into the tank they open and close the door several times to get its feel and location. Many people are introduced to floating at float centers. The best float result is achieved with the greatest reduction in distractions, including light, as long as that is comfortable for them. When the floater wants to get out, for whatever reason, and does not recognize the feel and location of the door easily, the center owner and the floater can be at risk.

Glenn

As we learned from our early floaters, many people have some fear about floating their first time: about it being too hot or too cold, being naked in an unfamiliar environment, being alone with themselves or something else. The most common fear expressed is claustrophobia. Often it is not just claustrophobia—though some people have that fear, too. It is the fear that they will have an experience that is difficult. Many of us have demons we are afraid will show up in the tank when we float, whether it is a hurt we endured, or how we hurt another, or something else we were unable to process at the time. The difference between the fearful people who will float and the ones who will not is the former have reason to believe there will be sufficient benefit from confronting the experience.

As Joe Rogan (actor, comedian, television host and host of The Joe Rogan Experience podcast) has said, "Imagine the joy and satisfaction that someone can get by dealing with some fear that they've had. They come and float and some fear that they have had, they deal with on their own and that creates a ripple through their life." We had one floater who, after the first few minutes, came out to the reception desk and asked for a chair to sit next to the tank the whole time. She came back the second day and did the same thing. On the third day she sat outside again. Then the fourth day she floated. Can you imagine the power she left with that she would have missed if we had tried to "manage" her fears away?

After we had floated for more than forty years, Lee and I floated in vertical tanks with an Epsom salt solution, created by Christopher Messer. Heavy ankle bracelets were used to keep the body vertical, and the buoyancy maintained the head above the solution. After floating for a while, I became terrified that I was going to suffocate. It made no reasonable sense since the tank had no cover and my head was in a large room with lots of air. In front of the tank there was a wet wooden deck where I could reach my arms out and rest them. Since it was easy to immediately lift myself up, I waited a moment even though I was terrified. Finally the fear was more than I wanted to deal with. I lifted myself up by pushing down on the deck, raising my chest out of the solution. I quickly took several deep breaths. Without the chest constriction I instantly felt better. I waited a few seconds and let myself back down into the solution. Almost immediately the terror returned, and I lifted myself up again. I repeated this process for about 20 minutes, each time working to remain in the solution longer. Though I did not completely handle the fear in this session, it was much less by the time I stopped.

Then, not long ago, I floated in our tank when the solution was a little warmer than I like. That always makes it seem stuffy to me. My nose happened to be stuffed up, so it was not easy to breathe through my nose. Amazingly, that old panic attack came back. I felt like I was going to suffocate. I put my towel in the door so it was open a crack, and laid down. I still was scared. I opened the door all the way and lay back down, and still I was scared. I got out. This was the choice that was most comfortable for me at that time. That evening when I went to bed I recalled the incident. I imagined being in that situation, felt the fear and stayed in the experience. I have done that a number of times since, each time until I fall asleep or cannot imagine the fear any longer. If I want to experience it and can't visualize the fear, I lightly squeeze my nose to bring it back. I know that if I create situations that allow me to confront the fear of suffocation, and eventually experience it fully, it will disappear. I soooo wish I had known this when I was young and scared of asking girls out.

Before I floated the first time, I was looking for some way to improve the quality of my life. I was not very happy, and I really did not like being in that state. I needed to change and, as a result of reading John Lilly's book, I thought floating might help. It became very important for me to float. I was willing to go through a lot of momentary, short term fear or discomfort for a higher quality of life forever after.

In John's workshops I discovered that every unprocessed physical or emotional trauma I walk around with limits the full range of my emotions and body. I had previously done a lot of folk dancing and swimming. I spent a couple of years being Rolfed, deep tissue work to remove traumas from my body. Thanks to Rolfing, I could now dance and swim with far more ease and grace using less energy. What a wonderful gift to the rest of my life in trade for some brief minor discomfort. Floating is also excellent at helping us learn to change our current state, with elegance. Andy Rush, a friend of ours who lived in an artist's community, bought one of our tanks for himself and his friends. Many in his community had fears that prevented them from floating. He found it useful to address fear at the beginning of an orientation he gave to first time floaters, which he shared with us. We have put more than twenty thousand floaters through the experience, and the orientation works well. We have found that we could never tell with certainty whether someone had fears. We give the orientation to everyone because of that, and because their friends may be afraid, and they may be able to repeat it to their friends. Even more important, as we have described above, floaters can have fears or panic attacks years after floating daily. They also need to know that it is important to use the tank comfortably, in their own way and at their own speed.

People who are afraid are most of all afraid of being afraid. We do not wish to remove people's fears, except their fear of being afraid. We think fear can be appropriate and is certainly common, and a person is not "less than" because they are afraid. Once they feel comfortable being afraid and are told that there is not a particular way to use the tank, and they are in control of using it in whatever way is comfortable for them, they are able to handle their own fears.

We do not want to take that away from them but, rather, give them the opportunity to grow. In the early years, we thought people would not realize maximum benefits from floating if they did not close the door. But over time we found they do benefit; however they use it. We also were concerned that when we talked about fear with people who were not afraid, they would become afraid. We have not noticed that happening ever.

Floating without distractions provides us with a situation where there is nothing present but us. This makes increasing our awareness far easier. Increased awareness gives us power and a more alive, easier, more productive life. We should not try to prevent floaters from having fear which can be dissolved by consciousness, by whatever way is comfortable, at each person's own rate of speed.

At the beginning of our orientation and any time we are talking to someone who expresses fear about floating, we say something like this: "Many people have fear or concern before they use the tank the first time, fear such as being alone in the dark, drowning, suffocation, claustrophobia, and others. The fears are usually the thought or idea that you will not be in control of the situation, but in this situation you are totally in control. You can get in and out of the tank whenever you want. You can leave a light on. You can leave the door totally open, you can keep it partially open with your towel, or you can close it. There is not a particular way to use it that is better than another way. Use it in whatever way is most comfortable for you."

Lee

When I introduce people to their first float, I always say, "Float in whatever way is comfortable for you." I have found that it is not enough to simply use the right words with the floater. I must actually be present when giving the orientation. When I have said it a lot, gotten tired of saying it, started saying it rotely, or have spaced out thinking about something else, my audience spaces out right along with me. Since people are very slow in functioning when they are afraid, which many people are before using the tank the first time, I give the orientation slowly and consciously enough that people will follow it.

If you have read the Samadhi Philosophy at the beginning and end of the book or the Why Float chapter, you have discovered that we do not believe in programming people or giving them our great ideas of how they can have a better float.

The following list includes all the important elements of our orientation based upon our experience since 1972 and our training with John Lilly.

What floaters should know before their first float.

Fears
1) Many people have fears.
2) Use it whatever way is comfortable.

Necessary physical data
3) How to find the door and recognize that it is the door.
4) There is plenty of air and where it enters.
5) If it is stuffy, it is because it is too warm. It can be made cooler by putting a towel in the door.
6) Ears will be underwater when floating. People who have had ear problems may want to use earplugs.
7) Demonstrate possible arm positions including support of the neck, if desired.
8) How to keep salt water out of the eyes and how to handle it if it happens.
9) Cuts and scratches will sting for a few minutes.
10) Remove contacts and jewelry.
11) How to operate all available in-tank controls: sound, light and temperature.
12) How they will know when their time is up.

Housekeeping concerns
13) How to not drip salt everywhere.
14) What to do after the float.

The orientation can be found in the appendix or online at the Samadhi Tank Co. Inc. Website.

CHAPTER NINE:
THE VERY FIRST FLOAT CENTER IN THE WORLD
BEVERLY HILLS
DESIGN AND MANIFESTATION

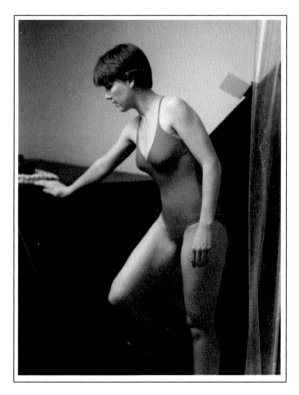

Ruth was not only our best model but also head of production in the factory.

Display tank in reception area.

Introduction

JCL was very clear about providing floating to the population of the world and we wanted to deliver what he was asking for. After four years in which we had set up two tanks in our home, we had learned how to introduce people to floating and developed ways of supporting their experiences in exploring this tool for their own use. We had designed two different tank models and now had a factory in place to manufacture and assemble them. We and John both wanted to get as many people as possible floating, and the business needed to have more of an income than the few tanks sold to some of the people coming to float at our home. If we could not sell more tanks, we would be out of business. We realized the amazing potential the tank provided for us and for the floaters who used it. How could we solve this problem? We were almost totally unknown. How do people do marketing?

Well, spas and hot tubs have retail outlets; stores where you can go to buy one. We could do that. We could provide a place where people float because when they do, some want to buy the tank. And by having them pay for their float we can cover our overhead. So that is what we decided to do. John thought it was a great idea. It aligned with his purpose: get more people floating.

Our Name

Dr. Lilly gave the company its name "Samadhi." Before we named our planned Center we were very concerned that our  name Samadhi would scare people away. It was so foreign: hard to pronounce, spell, and say. Would this be a barrier? Would it stop people from coming to float?

Six of us gathered on the carpet in front of our fireplace at home to brainstorm a name for our new Center. We started knowing that it was Dr. Lilly who gave us the name Samadhi, a Sanskrit word meaning a state of Being when the meditator becomes one with the object of meditation. From John Lilly's point of view, this is a state available by floating.

We started in the late afternoon. Some of us were concerned about whether we would damage the business by using a name people could not understand. Others were certain that being named by Dr. Lilly was the best ticket to success we could ever imagine, a spiritual name on top of that, so we would be silly not to call ourselves Samadhi. The third (and smallest) group just did not know what to think. They wanted to generate a brand-new group of good names and vote on them. We had tried that once a while back and the number of names connected to warm, wet, dark and quiet (our shortcut definition of the tank) was huge, it went on and on, and we could not choose one.

Finally, we got hungry and tired, it got dark, and we did not decide.

We continued to call our business, our company and our tank Samadhi, and we stopped thinking about whether to use the word or not. We had lots of other things to think about. In retrospect it was the best choice. People were curious about our name and what it meant. For some, floating in a dark box with an unusual, hard to pronounce name increased the intrigue. Since the late 60s, with increasing connectivity and global migration, we Americans have become more familiar with the sounds of distant languages. But in 1972 Sanskrit and other non-Germanic and non-Romance languages were astonishingly foreign. Samadhi was given to us, and we should have just said, "Thank You." And so we are known.

Finding the Center

What is a Center? How large or small should it be? What does it look like? Where do you put it? How much do we want to spend? Is floating the main activity of the center? Do we have something in addition to floating? How much space will that use? Who will be working in it? In the abstract these first questions made everything very complicated. No one had ever done this particular thing so we had nothing to copy. All we had was an idea, with no references.

John used to say, "In the province of the mind, what one believes to be true is true or becomes true within certain limits to be found experientially and experimentally. These limits are further beliefs to be transcended."

It was true that we did not know what steps to take. What did we know? Well, we knew we needed a place for the Center. What to do about that? Real Estate Broker: that is what we need. One of the people floating at our house was a real estate broker. We asked him to help.

This broker was an important teacher. There are many facets to renting business property that we did not know and finding someone who also had experience floating was even better since he understood something about our needs. We described our vision to him. The rules we had to obey were: not near a fire station, police station, or sports-gym. These could make a great deal of noise that might infiltrate the floating rooms in session. We drew a map around the area of Los Angeles where most of our floaters came from, excluding the more expensive neighborhoods. We wanted space for at least four tank rooms, each seven by twelve feet to contain a tank and shower and room to undress and dress.

The broker listened carefully and sent us to places as soon as they came on the market, filling us in on the good and bad elements of each. He taught us the things we needed to know about finding a good place. New questions came up: What did we like? What supported our vision? What was in fashion? How do we prioritize? A few weeks later he thought he had a place for us. He said "Beverly Hills." We said, "Uh oh... Expensive!" Yes, but, a separate building in the rear. Different! We discovered an empty two thousand square foot shell, with a concrete floor and glass door entry, currently in use as a Rolls Royce Repair Shop, going out of business. The size was perfect. It was unexpectedly different and good and not very expensive because it was in the rear. Not only did we get the place at a good price, but maybe being in the rear was to our advantage, a special new place with a sense of mystery.

It was special. People want to be cultural influencers, ahead of the curve, first, unique. We are on the right track! This is the mood we are looking for.

Lee - The Design

Next we learned building design. Of course, we wanted to do our own design. We were already experienced in what was needed, we liked to do everything ourselves, and we had many pictures in our minds' eyes.

Since the entry was obviously through the glass doors, we knew exactly where to place the welcome desk and reception area, which gave us the rear wall for floating, and that fit five tank rooms exactly. The welcome desk was placed to attract attention upon entering the Center. Before personal computers, we had a big appointment book for scheduling, and a phone because appointments were either called in or made in person. Our experience was that many appointments would have one change or another between the first contact and the actual float. Also at the desk was an electronic timing system we designed. Back then, although Glenn and I floated much longer, unless someone made a specific request we offered only one-hour floats.

It was a nice spot. With a southern exposure, the sun shone through the big glass windows all day. When you walked into the Samadhi Float Center, you were greeted by the staff at the welcome desk. Imagine it is your first float experience. You are walking to the display tank near the desk. We had learned that it is important to tell you that you are completely in control of your use of the tank and you can use it in whatever way is comfortable, e.g., door open or closed; arms above the head, behind the neck, at the sides. At the

Front desk for floaters entering and leaving.

Reception area where floaters could be before and after their float.

same time, we give you all the necessary safety and housekeeping instructions: keep salt from getting in your eyes, and off the walls, etc.

The orientation finished, we give you one or two towels and earplugs, press the timer switch for sixty-five minutes, and walk you behind the welcome desk to the hallway leading to one of the five tank rooms along the rear wall. Along our walk there are more doors and rooms. The first room behind the welcome desk is the Samadhi office. This is a good place for private conversations, on the phone or in person. The next room, with a refrigerator and stove where staff can take breaks, is also used to prepare for the many evening events. Next is a small space for laundry (mainly washing floaters towels). With a mop sink, this alcove is also the maintenance department workspace. Based upon our use and our square footage, the building department required two bathrooms, in those days one male and one female. They are the last rooms along the side of the building.

As we walk we talk. To increase your comfort level, I open the bathroom door where we see the toilet stall across the side of the room. On the other side is a four by six-foot wall-to-wall mirror for primping, with a shelf underneath to hold your personal supplies.

91

Since there could be five floaters in each session, I explain to you that you might meet other floaters. I tell you it is our experience that people sometimes meet while primping and form friendships and, of course, sometimes there is total silence. It is totally up to you. Those rooms became wonderful in so many ways that we never imagined. They were a strong attraction for repeat floats. For example, three friends could come at the same time to float and then hang out together in the bathroom. If the next session of floaters came out before the first group had moved to the common area, staff would bring them out.

I tell you that I will be responsible to let you know if it is time for you to come into the common area to make room for others at the end of their floats. Continuing on past the second bathroom, the hallway makes a right turn revealing the tank room entry doors. (The four years of learning at home were invaluable, and the first lesson was about salt. Anywhere there is a floatation tank, the main maintenance work is cleaning and preparing the tank and tank area between floats. A walk from a tank to a shower would result in inevitable salt drippings, leaving anywhere from a small to a really big mess. Any place the salt solution can drip, it will drip, making for a big clean up job. Thus, our five adjoining private rooms, each with its own walk-in shower connected to the front of the tank, are built to minimize the white Epsom salts crystal mess. We had mopped enough salty floors for at least a lifetime.)

A peek inside one of the five tank rooms with shower in front of tank.

Now in the room, I tell you that music will be your signal to get out of the tank. This is triggered by the timer set after the orientation, just before entering the hallway leading to the tank rooms. Once in a while someone would not hear the music so we were attentive for the twenty minutes it commonly took for the floater to emerge. When that happened, we would tiptoe into the room and knock on the side of the tank, hoping for a response: a splash, a grunt, anything. If that did not work, we would slowly open the door letting in a few inches of light and call their name. Once we had to open and close the door four times. (That was some float!)

Also from our experience, we learned that a prompt to transition out of the shower is helpful. We have had floaters space out and stay in the shower a really long time without some kind of signal. Our solution was an infrared heat lamp in the ceiling above the tank that turned on concurrently with the music, set for ten minutes. When the light went off, it silently and subtly signaled to end the shower. Showered and dried, you will walk back the short distance to the bathroom where you can use the facilities, attend to your hair, and so on, so the tank room is available for clean-up for the next float. I say, "When you are ready, please come have a cup of tea or check in at the front desk."

We solved the plastic not being light-proof.
Now we had a white tank we used for display.

We had a tea station, an electric tea maker with herbal teas that we formulated and brewed. It was on the opposite wall from the welcome desk, visible to everyone entering the room. Many floaters would pour themselves a cup and scan the area to see where they would like to spend their time. We found the tea station to be very useful for people coming out of their float and not sure what to do next. A staff person can approach them, or speak towards them asking, "Would you like a cup of tea?"

We still believe this is the most appropriate communication for the end of a float. This is so very useful and important. When people come out of their floats, if they are not rushing to another appointment, the "cup of tea" space gives them room to examine their experience simply, and as slowly as they wish. They can ask for something else when they are ready.

After accommodating all of the above, we were fortunate to have six hundred square feet left for all the functions we felt were useful after a float. We designed and made the furniture and arranged it to accommodate these different needs. One person could be in the back of the common area, sitting by themselves, unseen by others. Another might be drawing with pen and ink in a book they would leave for others to see. Someone else might be speaking with a staff person, perhaps ordering a tank. A fourth could have headphones, listening to music. A curious visitor might be examining the display tank in the room. And, of course, there was the tea station.

We were very proud of our creation, with a strong feeling that some intelligence greater than ours had collaborated in the work of building this Center where life became greater than we expected. We were supported in creating a space to be present. I was studying the John Lilly book Dyadic Cyclone at the time, and John talks about the importance of the happiness of the dyad; in our case the dyad being the Glenn/ Lee relationship. He wrote that the male/ female dyad is a very strong unit. This is how we were. The Center was an amazing piece of work that worked beyond our imagination.

Staff

Each staff person performed any of the many jobs required. At the welcome desk they made the many changes, booked new appointments, answered questions, took payment, and attended to anything else that might, would, could, and did come up. There was always a maintenance person to check the tank rooms after each float, do the laundry, sometimes answer the phone, check the teapot and check supplies in the reception area. We learned that with four or more tanks we needed to have at least two people working the Center at all times. With the many jobs, the mood of the center was more welcoming when the staff could be present, performing peacefully.

When all five tanks were in use, the maintenance person would prepare the tank room for the next floater as soon as it was empty: opening the tank door to inspect for anything left behind, quickly wiping down anything in the room in need, letting the front desk know which room was ready for the next floater, then repeat. Most of our electrical and plumbing service people bartered floats for their work. That suited us in both our mission and our budget. A win all the way around.

In those pre-personal computer days we had developed a "User Card" that had space for personal information. On the card we wrote any matters of note. For example, if they had floated through the music signal necessitating our entry into the room, we would remind them of what happened and ask for permission to knock sooner. Some floaters had no idea that they had not heard anything. We got permission to open the door and do what was needed to let them know their time was up. Often they offered up a good suggestion which we were happy to use. People know their own habits.

The place was extraordinary. The atmosphere maintained a feeling of support and caring that welcomed all who entered. I have only told you a small number of things about this center, and I do not want to sound as if we did not make any mistakes. The biggest one came so early. It must have been a warning that if we had arrived in Heaven, we still had to pay attention. No going to sleep on the job! Ana who worked at the Center was excellent in being with floaters. Beautiful! A perfect job. After the first week, as we were reviewing how we were doing, we noticed that Ana had not made any user cards. We knew there were many things to do, so I went to Ana and spoke to her about it. She became quiet. And then told me she had never learned to read and write. That left me without speech! How did we neglect to ask? What is our responsibility with those who come to help? In the places we take care of, we have to take care of everything! No blame: just, our full attention required!

Promotion

Not only did we have to build a Center, we had to promote it. Because we were doing something unique and newsworthy, we looked for a public relations person rather than an advertising agency. We were lucky enough to find someone who, wanting a tank for himself, was willing to trade for his work. He was well connected in the world of creative endeavors of the moment, including fashion, and he used his contacts very well for us. We learned a great deal from him.

Three months after we opened there was a story about us on the front page of the City section of the *Los Angeles Times*. From then on, we were filled to capacity. When we were filled to capacity, we sold five to ten tanks each month.

Other Center Activities

Weekly, Thursday evenings we offered the "night flight" to teachers, therapists, clubs, and families that wanted a group of five tanks available from 10:00 PM to 7:00 AM to use in their practice/ studies/ teaching. It was very popular and continued the entire time we were there.

John and Toni Lilly at opening party.

We had an agreement with John Lilly that when forty people signed up and paid for a workshop with him, he would come. That was very special. I do not remember any other group that was so lucky. It provided a very simple way of learning the ideas of this often unavailable scientist. He and Toni got that room buzzing!

96

We were primarily manufacturers, and our purpose in opening our center was twofold. The first was to sell tanks, which we were accomplishing, around a hundred tanks per year. The second objective was to spread floating. After the first four months of operation we stayed filled to capacity. Then, to our surprise, people started asking us how they could start a center like ours.

Glenn was an excellent inventor. Lee was excellent at listening to others. He designed a tank. She worked on introducing people to it. We worked together, clear about our direction. Our skills were growing. We knew how to design, build, and sell a tank and how to design, build, and operate a center. The next thing we needed to learn was how to sell one.

CHAPTER TEN

FLOATING AND CULTURAL CREATIVES
UNDERSTANDING OUR MARKET

Oz Fritz with Soundboard
photo credit: John Taber

Inside a floatation tank

Being with floaters coming through the center in Beverly Hills, it seemed to us that everyone enjoyed floating. But after a while we realized that was not true. We noticed that the people who came to float all had a spiritual bent to them, not necessarily obvious, but at some level.

A member of the American bobsled Olympic team being trained in Lake Placid, New York, called. He had purchased a tank a couple of years earlier and had been in communication with us about it, but this time it was something different. "I'm going to be in California with a sports chiropractor friend of mine, also involved in the Olympics, and we would like to take you out to lunch." We were excited about expanding the conversation about floating into a wider realm, especially the sports world.

They started the lunch by saying they never had an opportunity to talk to their acquaintances about spiritual matters and wanted to finally have a chance to talk with us. We were surprised when they wanted to talk about spirituality. We were learning that the spiritual journey can be accessed through the conscious performance of any endeavor.

The next year we did a market research study at the Beverly Hills Center to study the nature of the floating market. We wanted and needed to know who our people were. We found a professor of marketing from the University of Nevada at Reno to conduct focus groups with the floaters in our center. The results were very interesting. He found an "emerging market segment" of people interested in self-actualization that he called "Cultural Creatives."

In the late 1970s a Stanford University psychology professor, Dr. Paul H. Ray, conducted research looking at marketing segments, not from the view of demographics but from the view of people's values. He believed people acted based upon their values. He discovered a new emerging group with a value system different from the existing dominant population. That dominant population he termed "moderns." Their values were personal success and financial gain. They accepted things as they were and found material consumption rewarding.

Amazingly, the history of the "moderns" can be traced to 1555 when the first major joint stock company, the Muscovy Company, was formed in England. Muscovy was an area around Moscow, Russia, and the company had a monopoly on trade between this area and England. Many of the first joint stock companies were trading companies. For example, the Hudson Bay Trading Company, started by two Frenchmen in England, was created to achieve a fur trading monopoly in that region of northern Canada drained by all rivers and streams flowing into the Hudson Bay. This area comprised over one-third of the area of modern-day Canada and, in the 19th century, became Canada's largest land "purchase."

In the seventies the Cultural Creatives were just developing in society. According to Dr. Ray, their interest was spiritual and psychological development. They saw the world holistically and were interested in creating a better way of life. Other values important to them were authenticity, social activism, ecology, and social justice. They were divided into two major groups: half were concerned with the environment and the other half spiritual and personal growth. The latter were the ones interested in floating.

Before 2010, there was barely a mention of Cultural Creatives in the mainstream media, which may explain a very curious attribute. Each felt isolated and did not realize their power. However, their overall size grew from their participation in movements from the sixties to the present including the hippies, civil rights, antiwar, feminism, gay rights, and many others.

Imagine you have just discovered roses: the smell, the shape, the color. As your interest grows the world becomes a flower wonderland. So the interest in social justice expanded consciousness into the larger world.

In 1980, when the study was done in our center, the cultural creatives made up three percent of the population. According to Dr. Ray and Sherry Ruth Anderson, PhD., in *The Cultural Creatives: How 50 Million People Are Changing the World*, in 1999 they comprised twenty-six percent and, by 2008, were more than thirty-five percent of the world population. *In Occupy World Street*, 2012, Ross Jackson, PhD. reflects that they represented a truly significant shift in values, going on "below the radar screens of the media" which has barely mentioned them at the same time that all the huge companies do much of their promoting to them.

Laura Sydell, of NPR radio said, "Even under Apple founder Steve Jobs, the company did emphasize values. Remember the Think Different ad campaign that used pictures of the Dalai Lama, Amelia Earhart, Mahatma Gandhi?" The identification of the Cultural Creatives helped us clarify the market for the tank. People who make floating a part of their life are those who can see the benefit and really seek that benefit in their life. When I came out of the tank the first time, in that more conscious state, I found I was completely comfortable talking to others. I had to have a tank for myself.

When we consider the number of people who are reluctant to use the floatation tank, from outright fear to the inconvenience of needing to shower both before and after, it is important to realize that people need to see significant benefits. As with all unfamiliar environments, there is a comfort and learning curve. Many people do not fully understand it immediately. It can take several introductory floats to become at one with the tank experience, to make friends with ourselves and the environment. We have often considered doing away with single first float sessions to instead offer a three or five-float package as the introduction. Many floaters have had unremarkable initial experiences who later go on to have meaningful experiences and even make or purchase their own tank.

The floatation tank center owning industry has appealed to many people including those only interested in catching the next "big wave" with no intrinsic interest in floating itself. These latter are trying to make a business when they are not the market, i.e., not Cultural Creatives. Without needing to float themselves, they do not know the state of consciousness that is possible from floating. Our concern is that when their business fails, giving the industry a bad name, the issue is really the mismatch. These are people who open a float facility without understanding the real benefits.

The state of consciousness available from floating, better understood in Tibet and India, is not generally talked about in this culture. It can take time for floaters to become familiar with the state of being present, to notice the subtle differences between present and their normal state. Floating is not the easiest industry to make money in if you are not a strong spiritual cultural creative. Business consultants, who may not know the state of being conscious, have inappropriately steered "moderns" into this business, more interested in the material universe than spiritual development.

We are filled with constant mental chatter about things left undone in the past and how we should be spending our time and energy in the future. When we give these things time to unreel, our mind quiets down.

As we were completing this book Mary Crosby, a true cultural creative, purchased her second tank from us. When asked how she used the tank she responded:

I have not had the pleasure of having a tank in several years but I had one for many and it was the deepest quiet both internally and externally that I have experienced. Physically, because I was so buoyant, it was incredibly restful for my body. I greatly look forward to having that gift in my life again.

We work so hard to find peace and quiet and rest be it with meditation or yoga or hiking or nature and with the tank, for me, it felt like I was able to skip through many steps and simply get to the heart of quiet.

Pretty difficult to verbalize the impact - It's such an intensely personal experience but that's a bit of how I feel.
Warmly, Mary

Most of us do not know when we are awake or present. Floaters often describe being present by saying they are relaxed. We are all familiar with being present such as when we need to learn something or when we get completely immersed in an activity we enjoy, when we do a rigorous sport, or when we are in awe of an incredible nature scene. Characteristics of being present or awake are when our concentration is focused on the present moment, a sense that we can deal with whatever arises in the situation, an experience of present time continuously unfolding, a space of heightened and dispassionate observation with a sense of peace, well being and love.

This is the altered state I was in when I got out of the tank the first time. To varying degrees, it is the state many of us are in when we finish floating if we do it long or often enough. The more we move into being present, being in our heart, spirit, or the flow, the more we are there in the rest of our life. If you want to develop a muscle or a skill, the more you use it, the more you have it. *Moving repeatedly into the present moment becomes a magnet to pull other things to us that in turn move us to being present.* So we become more functional and balanced. When difficult events happen in our life, we are available to deal with them with ease. We see them with more clarity and less automatic reaction. Since we are not in an ego state, our ego is not hurt.

As mentioned previously, John Lilly referred to ECCO as determining the long term coincidences (synchronicity) and we ourselves are responsible for the short term ones. Forty some odd years later I think I finally understand some of this. It resolves something my mother and I would talk about when I was in high school, in the kitchen while she was cooking dinner. "Is life predetermined or do we determine it?" "Is there free will?"

This brings us to something in our lives that suggests ECCO may have known Lee and I were going to get together and work with John's tank *10 years before the tank was invented.*

John Lilly invented the tank in 1954. When I was born, in 1941, my father raised foxes for their pelts. Each year, in New York City, there was an annual auction of the yearly supply of American fox pelts. In 1944, three years after I was born, my father sold a pelt to the I. J. Fox company for the most money that a pelt sold for that year. The year before John invented the tank, I wrote an essay in junior high school describing my father achieving that distinction. Then, twenty years later, in 1974, I met Lee and we started the tank business. The next year I found the essay and showed it to Lee. She said, "The pelt that your father sold in 1944 was to my sister's and her husband's company, I. J. Fox."

My father had dealings with Lee's sister's company thirty years before Lee and I met. I wrote the essay one year before John invented the tank. ECCO determines the long term coincidences and we are responsible for the short ones, which brings me to an observation: When we decide to follow the flow of ECCO's path, events go very well for us. When we go against the current, they go less well. When we work for ECCO, magic happens.

ECCO (Earth Coincidence Control Office) was very kind to us, which happens when you are going in the direction she is going. Our location in Beverly Hills was convenient to the entertainment industry. Although not everyone in the entertainment industry is a cultural creative, I think it is safe to say that many in the industry would consider themselves on the cultural creative end of the spectrum.. This put us in the midst of the best place on the planet for our potential customers. One example is a TV editor who came into the center on a Sunday afternoon with the challenge of cutting twenty seconds from his thirty-minute program. Part way through his float he showed up at the reception desk, asked to borrow the phone, called his studio and told them where to make the change. Another example is Michael Crichton. He handled his writer's block floating at the center, then found floating so useful that he bought a tank for his home. His books have gone on to sell over two hundred million copies worldwide. In all, he tallied forty-five writing credits: novels, screenplays, and documentaries.

Both of these are examples of floaters who drew great benefit from the tank. Both used it for creativity and one of them, in discovering himself, discovered the source of his block.

Our close friend, Oz Fritz, a recording engineer with a long-term working relationship with Oysterhead, told us they had written and recorded a song in 2001 about him and his floating, "Oz is Ever Floating." A week after the telling, we got an email with the following attached:

Oz Is Ever Floating

I came to be known by my peers in the music industry as the guy who floats; my enthusiasm for daily dips in the floatation tank was known far and wide. At an Oysterhead session in Phish's rustic recording barn, Les

Claypool teased, "Are you going to jump into the tank as soon as you get home, Oz?"

"He'll probably dive in before even saying hello to anyone," chimed in an assistant engineer. Playing along I said, "That's exactly what I'll do!"

The next day I caught Les staring at me from the other side of the studio before furiously scribbling something down on paper. The songwriting process for Oysterhead (Les Claypool, Stewart Copeland and Trey Anastasio) was to jam for hours on end, musically improvising grooves and breaks while recording everything onto 24 track analog tape. These tracks would then get transferred into Pro Tools for editing. Musically interesting sections would be noted, with the best ones becoming the basis for a song. Very soon after watching Les watch me, I recorded him singing the first draft of a song that would become "Oz Is Ever Floating." The next line was something abstract that made no sense and would be changed. It went something like: "to the things that don't mean much to a tree." After that initial recording Les took a break to write some more lyrics. To find some inspiration he asked me how I used the tank. Of course, I've experimented with floating in many different ways over the years; I answered what came to my mind that moment, "I use the tank to prepare for death. I use it to get a sense of what it might be like for my consciousness to continue surviving without a body." Les quickly found some words and we put the new verse down on tape. He sang through an empty roll of toilet paper to create a natural filter for his voice giving it an edge that made it stand out. The music ended up sounding like Primus-style progressive funk rock.

I thought this song could be a great promotion for floating. After the Oysterhead album was recorded, but before it was mixed, everyone took a break and went back to their respective home locales. I had been asked to mix the album, but had to reluctantly turn it down, unfortunately, as the schedule would conflict with dates already reserved *to record Tom Waits. I asked and received permission from the band to play a rough mix of "Oz Is Ever Floating" for Glenn and Lee Perry. After they heard it, they asked me if they could show it to John Lilly with whom they planned to visit the following week. Playing unreleased, unfinished music is always tricky so I called up Les and cleared it with him. Les wanted to know who John Lilly was. I told him he was the scientist who first came up with the concept of sensory deprivation isolation that would eventually manifest as floating in a floatation tank. After returning from their visit, the Perrys reported that John —only a few weeks away from permanently exiting his biological shell—loved the song, but had no idea what it meant.*

A month or so later I heard the final mix and discovered that Les had researched John Lilly. He modified the song, changing the lyric about a tree to mention Dr. John C. Lilly. Having great respect and admiration for John Lilly, as well as for the members of Oysterhead, I felt greatly honored for inspiring this song; a highlight of my career. It not only publicized floating in a fun and groovy way, it also made a new and unlikely population demographic aware of John Lilly and floating. "Oz Is Ever Floating" is the second track on the Oysterhead album The Grand Pecking Order. There is also an excellent performance of it from Conan O'Brien's late night show that can be found on YouTube.

We received the email from Oz in June, 2019. The next day, we received the following from Ryan and Talia Chaffee of Fadeaway Floatation in Des Moines, Iowa:

Hi Glenn and Lee,

I just wanted to reach out and thank you and Lee for what you do.

It seems we only reach out when something goes wrong.

I appreciate all the help and quick responses the past few years when something has gone awry. You guys have been a joy to work with!

I also enjoy when I'm explaining what type of tanks we have that I can state that you have been making them since like 1972! The true original! And the connection and history with Dr. Lilly. Which is how I first heard of floating...in a song about Oz Is Ever Floating and Dr. John C. Lilly.

I hope all is well with you and thank you both!
Ryan Chaffee

ECCO at work.

CHAPTER ELEVEN

THE SAN FRANCISCO CENTER
A CLASH OF VALUES

San Francisco Center Seating

Demo shower and tank, Front desk, San Francisco Center

Glenn

We were the first commercial floatation tank manufacturer and the first floatation tank center designers and operators. Our job was to have as many people as possible floating, going along with John Lilly's idea in *Center of the Cyclone*, of saving the human species. Some of our customers began thinking about having a center like ours. It never occurred to us that anyone would want their own center since our purpose with the center was to familiarize people with floating and to encourage them to own their own tanks, all in the service of increasing consciousness. Would this be our next pursuit?

Attending many Dr. Lilly workshops helped develop an attitude of exploring the world in general and consciousness in particular. By floating daily we expanded our explorations of ourselves and our universes. Lee, by introducing and being with floaters over time, was exploring how to interact with them, and by us talking about their conversations after they left we made it all more conscious. It seemed that we were approaching everything from the point of beginner's or Zen mind. And we were using LSD to explore other states of consciousness.

As Laurie helped us edit this chapter, she asked questions to get clear about what we really wanted to accomplish. She, by exploring, by coming from beginner's mind, allowed a new understanding to spring forth. We realized that business has been a spiritual practice for us. Though I have always been a problem solver and therefore an asker of questions, John's workshops gave me a greater insight into this approach.

When floaters told us they wanted to open their own centers, we forgot our beginner's mind. We turned our backs on our very strength, a lapse that got us into trouble. We were seen as talking to wonderful people all day: laughing, smiling, having a really good time. It was exactly the kind of spiritually fulfilling work many were looking for. As a matter of fact, two young men asked if they could work at the center. We were full up on staff and told them so. They decided to open their own two-tank center. We gave them our blessing. They went on to sell lots of Samadhi tanks and, as the years went by, their center expanded to six tanks.

We began participating in the Whole Earth Expos, trade shows for new and different products in the fields of health, lifestyle, and consciousness. The event producers were looking to give the audience an experience and, boy, did we have one. The floatation tank was new, and different from the other products. This provided a great opportunity for people to see and touch them, and even try floating before buying. The Expo venues had dressing rooms with showers, which, at other times were used during performances by actors or athletes, where we set up two tanks ready for floating. After the first morning, word spread about the opportunity to float in a Samadhi Tank. To allow as many people as we could to have a small taste we offered only half-hour sessions. (1-hour sessions were the norm at the Beverly Hills center at that time.) We were fully booked. The first to book were the booth owners who loved having a tiny respite during a very strenuous day. Their hair, wet from the shower identified them, and their fresh energy and easy smiles made them stars in the show, with the Samadhi Tank as the energy source.

We were the right people at the right time. We were totally lucky, and totally exhausted. Now we were looking for someone to assist us in getting clear about how to help others open their own centers. "Someone" found us. We were at the Whole Earth Expo in San Francisco with the idea that we could find someone there. Before the end of the second day, George (not his real name) introduced himself as one of our satisfied tank owners. He was a very successful and charismatic businessman, vice president of a division of the fastest growing American leasing company, who would be happy to help us in any way he could. Glenn and I exchanged one of those "problem solved" looks.

We explained ourselves and our need for help. He lived an hour away by air and was willing to show up for dinner any day we called. He was eager and happy to work with us. We went home and over the next week agreed we wanted his input. George floated often, and we appreciated this about him. We were clear there were people who wanted their own centers. We saw this as a "problem" we were unable to solve. How could we help them? Over dinner we described the situation, and he offered to reflect on it and get back to us with a solution.

He developed a plan for a floatation tank franchising company. He had been to our Beverly Hills Center, and he suggested we become partners in the new venture. We asked for advice from a lawyer friend, who, after researching the "opportunity," advised us to go in another direction. We did not follow the lawyer's advice. George's vision for the Samadhi Alliance was a 20-tank showroom center in San Francisco. His interest was selling franchises. We, on the other hand, were excited by the vision of making floating more widely available in the world, the opportunity to train center staff, and new centers selling lots of tanks.

Seating in San Francisco Center

George raised a million dollars from limited partners. Our contribution to the Alliance was our Beverly Hills center, and the knowledge of how to build and run centers and train franchisees. The Samadhi Tank Company, apart from the Alliance, would supply the tanks to the franchisees. They would sell floating as well as tanks. The Samadhi Alliance rented a floor at 2001 Van Ness Avenue in San Francisco and built a 20-tank center, with room left for an auditorium.

George was a mix of cultural creative and modern. He loved floating and his main interest was in big business and big marketing.

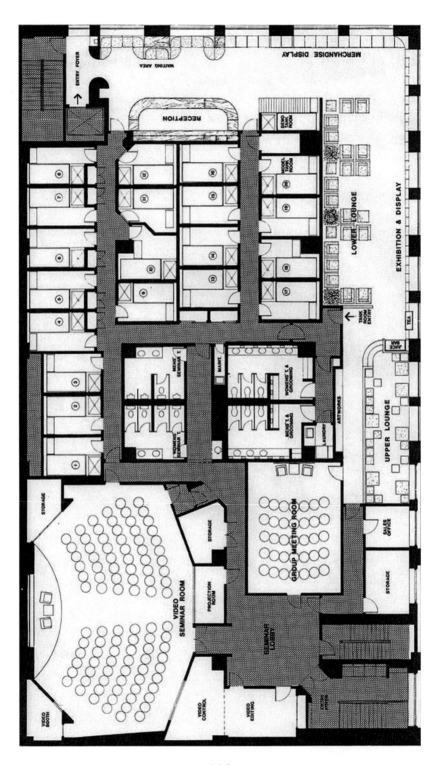

116

RECEPTION AND LOUNGE

SAMADHI CENTER · SAN FRANCISCO, CALIFORNIA

We now see that his main objective was to get people to buy franchises, demonstrating the "modern" values of personal success and financial gain. Our goal was getting people to float, in line with our cultural creative roots. There was some tension between him and us centered around our spiritual orientation and his money focus. The center ended up a showcase of wealth, comfort and glitz. That did not feel right to us. George chose the location thinking the jet-lagged airline personnel staying in the hotels within walking distance would float. Unfortunately, they were not yet ready. They were not the Cultural Creatives the floatation tank attracted. The floating traffic at the Center was low.

George worked very hard but had an Achilles heel: high overhead. He paid himself a salary of $9,000 a month. This was 1980, and we said, "This is a little bootstrap operation! Your pay is just too much." He said, "Okay, I am going to cut back as best I can." And he worked really hard to reduce his salary by $500 a month. The place lasted only one year. This endeavor was a lot more difficult than we had anticipated. He sold only four franchises, not enough to support the operation. The Samadhi Alliance ended up in bankruptcy with three quarters of a million dollars in debt. The center contents were put up for auction. That was one big beautiful premature idea. We believe the operation would have had a better chance of success if the focus had been toward cultural creatives.

In this period the Alliance was the major purchaser of our tanks. Unfortunately, most of the tanks they "bought" were not yet paid for, and we lost about $120,000 in 1980 dollars. Our Beverly Hills Center was invested in the Alliance partnership so, with the bankruptcy, the Center was lost. We came out of this with our experience of creating and running a wonderful Center for a few years, and a Center Operations Manual in which we captured our methods and procedures. We still had our manufacturing company, the Samadhi Tank Company. Other than that we were back at ground zero with no operating capital and no ready outlet for selling tanks.

Operating and running the Beverly Hills center was Lee's calling. Losing it was very painful to her. It took a while to process the grief. ECCO had other plans for us. This was not the end of our story.

It was what we needed to seriously think about our future. We had promised each other that as soon as we had tank production handled, we could leave the city. John Lilly talked about "Coincidence Control." If you live right, the coincidences will build up for you in unexpected and surprising and beneficial ways. If they do not build up, you are not living right and had best examine your way of life. After taking a good hard look and examining our way of life carefully, we decided it was time to leave Los Angeles. We finally did this in 1989 after a great deal of conversation and research.

San Francisco Center Closing

CHAPTER TWELVE
PICKING OURSELVES BACK UP
NEW DESIGNS, F.T.A. AND AIDS

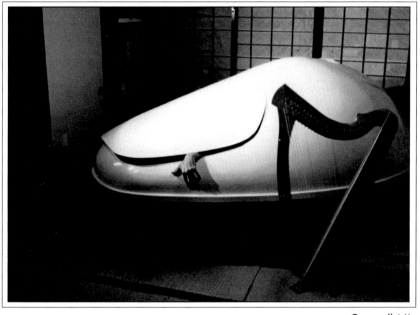

Samadhi II

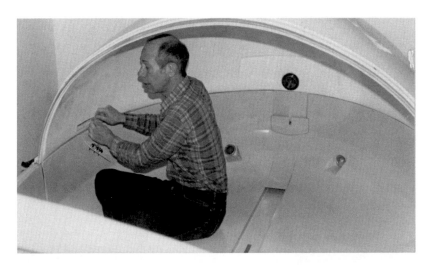

Installing and evaluating the Samadhi II

Lee

Even though we had lost all of our sales outlets, luckily there had been an amazing amount of free publicity: in magazines, newspapers and on television and radio. What we learned is that public relations (PR) begets PR. All of the media are looking to each other for content. During the early 1980s, there was a lot of interest in floating.

The tank is difficult to photograph for publicity. In 1983 we worked with an extraordinarily talented photographer for the book, *24 Hours in the Life of L.A.* One hundred photographers were assembled to capture a slice of a day in the life of the City of Los Angeles. This had been successfully done in London and the publisher was giving it another try.

Interested in photographing the tank as representative of the spirit of Los Angeles, particularly because both the tank inventor and manufacturer lived there, Horst, a German photographer, contacted us five days before the shoot. We considered many ideas for pictures. Finally, our plan was to substitute one of the regular sides of a tank with clear Plexiglass to be able to see inside. Floating in this tank would be an obviously pregnant woman. The idea was that the mother was the vessel in which the fetus was floating, the Samadhi tank was the vessel in which the mother was floating, and the tank was floating in the ocean. Our meeting supplied the necessary enthusiasm to get the project going. We must have had some visions of fame and fortune to accept a task of that magnitude. In addition to finding a way to get a tank with warm water set up on some beach at six o'clock in the morning, we had very few days to find a very pregnant model willing to be published in a book, naked in a floatation tank, with a bunch of strangers.

Getting the tank solution was quite simple. Our accountant was living in what is called "The Colony" at Malibu Beach. He owned one of our tanks. For those of you who do not know, there are seven hundred pounds of Epsom salt dissolved in each Samadhi tank, which allows people to float, and is quite valuable. It is not the kind of thing you just throw away. We needed to pump the solution to the beach in front of the house from the second-floor rear of a house up on concrete piers. We needed the solution to be kept warm for our model's comfort. The beach is often chilly in the early morning hours and we wanted the face in the photograph to be peaceful and serene, not frozen and brave.

Getting a model seemed impossible at first. Once the strategy was found, the job was simple. A tank owner in Los Angeles had just given birth. We called her, explained the problem and asked for her help. She recommended that I call her Lamaze teacher who might help us find someone. The Lamaze teacher immediately thought of three women and predicted that one of the three might be quite interested. Lucky coincidence? Susan Ragsdale, artist, was three or four weeks from delivering her first child and was familiar with the tank since she had floated at the Beverly Hills Samadhi Center. She welcomed the chance to have her nude photograph in an art book. She thought it would be a good experience for her and a memorable experience for her unborn child. She appeared at 6 A.M. with her lunch and towels and a blanket and very good spirits.

Way before dawn we were pumping water through a series of seven hoses into our modified tank located on the beach. We had made a Plexiglass side and siliconed it in place. By the time we had four of the ten inches of water pumped in, we noticed some dark sand at the corner. We had a leak. We were worried about losing so much water that the photograph would show the model floating too close to the bottom. We never thought of bringing extra salt in case we needed to add buoyancy. In the picture she is floating too low but the photo is so spectacular that no one notices.

Horst, the photographer wanted to begin shooting at 6 A.M. because the light was best at that hour. When the sun cracked over the horizon we upped our speed (which was already very fast). This was a once in a lifetime opportunity. Some distance from the side of the tank a trench was dug so the lens of the camera was straight on the surface of the solution which was at the level of the ocean at the horizon. He used a big Hasselblad on a tripod. His assistant took many meter readings from various points in an arc around the tank. We were instructed how to sweep the sand. We found a way to hold the door open at the angle Horst wanted. After those things were done, the model went into the tank and Horst directed her through many different positions, always checking that she was comfortable in the pose. He was a perfectionist's perfectionist. Never ever before had we worked alongside someone so precise. I felt like I was in a cathedral. He invoked a feeling of worship of excellent work habits. The photo was chosen to be in the introduction to the book. It also appeared as a centerfold in the German magazine, *Stern* and the *Paris Match*. It remains an iconic photograph in the annals of floatation. (Editor: See a version in the center color section.)

By this time there were four other manufacturers promoting their tanks which also helped get the word out about the wonders of floating. In an industry so new, education was paramount. Competition was immaterial. The four other manufacturers were Float to Relax, Ova, Floatarium and Oasis. Float to Relax went public and did not last long. Ova's tank dimensions were small, and they never gained enough of a market. Floatarium had a fire which closed them down. Oasis is still in business today. These four manufacturers all used fiberglass for the bodies of their tanks.

Glenn

Samadhi flirted with fiberglass over the years but never found it satisfactory for several reasons. First, it is toxic to produce, an important issue for me with my high environmental sensitivity. Additionally, because fiberglass is very heavy the door requires hydraulic cylinders which have a possibility of failure, slight but higher than Samadhi is comfortable with. It is also very difficult to make light-proof, especially around the door where tongue and groove is required.

I received a letter from Douglas Fir, a young North American inventor living in Japan, who was designing a commercial float tank. Previously he had designed a bicycle powered forklift. He asked for our help with the design and marketing. We agreed and worked with him long distance which, of course, pre-internet, was not the ideal design situation. Douglas handled the finances and production. Once it was close to completion, and he had found a company to manufacture them, surprisingly out of fiberglass, he brought me to Japan to review the design and see the factory.

At the same time, a Canadian, Rod Punnett, after reading an article by Michael Hutchison about floating in the March 1984

New Age Journal, said to himself, "This is it!" He traveled around the United States, floating in different centers, including coming to visit us in Los Angeles. Later, Glenn sent him a picture of a prototype of the new tank. He loved how it looked and immediately placed his order for four and began designing a float center in his home city of Vancouver, Canada.

Two months later five absolutely gorgeous tanks arrived at our factory in Los Angeles. We called it the Samadhi II. We immediately set one up in our home and started floating in it daily, taking a very critical look at the design. There were thirteen items we thought either needed to be corrected or improved. Although it was a hard, painful decision to make, we finally concluded that some of the items could not be corrected satisfactorily. The two most difficult problems to fix were getting the filtration system to work properly and making it lightproof. There were several others nearly as difficult. We thought one of the problems might have been that the production crew in Japan, who had a very good reputation, had no idea what they were making. It did not look like anything they were familiar with and they had no mental picture of its use.

As Rod Punnett's center, Threshold, was being completed, we shared with him the problems we had found. He was confident he could make the Samadhi II work for him. Rod brought Lee and Toni Lilly to the opening of his center which occurred at the same

Glenn in Samadhi II

126

time as the conference they attended together in Vancouver. Once his center opened, he became an avid member of the Floatation Tank Association (F.T.A.). After his center closed, Rod came to Los Angeles, stayed with us, and became the administrator of the F.T.A.

The industry was very busy. John Turner, Jr., PhD., and Thomas Fine, LSW, both at the Medical College of Ohio, were performing research using one of our tanks. In 1981, together with Peter Suedfeld, Dean of Psychology, University of British Columbia, they conducted Restricted Environmental Stimulation (REST): A Workshop and Experience, presenting REST in psychological, physiological and therapeutic perspectives. IRIS, the International REST Investigators' Society was formed in 1983 to bring together the growing community of researchers and therapists interested in the effects of stimulus reduction. The first IRIS conference was held in Denver in 1983. The second conference, in 1985, was in New Orleans. Programs for the IRIS conferences included papers across the spectrum of environments characterized by stimulus reduction.

Lee

Alma Daniels bought one of our first commercial tanks and had it installed in her beautiful apartment overlooking Central Park in New York City. Her organization, the "Human Potential Counseling Service," was dedicated to helping people transform their lives, and she understood the potency of floating as a tool both for herself and her practice. In 1983 she created the F.T.A., a nonprofit trade organization originally created, and continuing to serve, floatation tank manufacturers and tank center owners. With her skills in organization, communication, and advertising, the F.T.A. grew quickly. She was instrumental in the publicity gathering around the business of floating.

The New Orleans IRIS conference included commercial tank manufacturers, personal users and floatation tank center owners in addition to the medical and scientific community, together with anyone else wanting to be part of this growing industry. As a special bonus, John Lilly gave the keynote address. On the commercial side, it was very exciting for us to be part of giving this new industry a form. The scientists were concerned that joining with the commercial section would not be accepted by the science-based organizations as it could be interpreted as a conflict of interest. It was decided that the two groups would meet in separate locations to allow each the adequate work time to address their needs and move their agendas forward.

For six years the F.T.A. held annual conferences in different cities around the USA. There was always a keynote speaker after which the participants formed groups to share the previous year's activities and to brainstorm building an international organization interested in promoting industry-wide growth. The results were long term friendships among the Centers, and the spread of successful ideas and best practices. We had a really good idea, floating, to share with the world. Through IRIS and the F.T.A. an industry was born, nourished by the science and commercial interests working independently in community.

In 1984 John gave a four-day workshop at Feathered Pipe Ranch in Helena, Montana. He invited us to bring a tank to be available twenty-four hours a day for his students to experience. This was my first John Lilly workshop. There were about twenty-five students. I was excited to learn his curriculum and expand my connection to his teaching. Students of his had floated at our house in the early days, and I had been impressed with them. They were practicing appreciators: serious, attentive and curious.

The Ranch had a lodge with accommodations for workshops and retreats. There was a small one-room out-building with a shower, where we set up the tank. Away from the lodge there was a flat, grassy area with chairs for the lectures. There was a table with the first Apple computer; that funny little box that was the beginning of personal computing.

In addition to lectures by Dr. Lilly, there was a balance beam to promote physical awareness and a small, supervised vegetable garden to encourage growing healthy food. We gave information about floating, including how to sign up and a short orientation. The tank was available 24/7, and all slots were filled on the first day. I had never been to a workshop like this. Each was free to follow their own interests, and together we were learning computer science, responsibility for our bodies, caring for garden vegetables,

Floating

Double Issue 1989

Floating

Premier Issue   Fall

Floating

Premier Issue   Fall, 1987

Making photo for the cover of Floating Magazine issue 1

relationships, and anything else each of us wanted to learn from Dr. Lilly. For me, computer science was the most striking. Here we were, on a ranch in Montana, and there was a computer. I thought computers required big cities. I was inducted by John Lilly into an area that was completely foreign and encouraged to touch and learn. Shortly thereafter we found ourselves the owners of one of those computers.

Floating Magazine

In early 1987 the F.T.A. Board decided that an F.T.A. magazine would be good for the industry. Since Samadhi had recently bought the brand new Macintosh computer, we offered to take this on. We published three issues of a new magazine, *Floating*. The first was in the fall of 1987, the second in the winter of 1987/1988 and the third was a double issue published in the fall of 1989.

By 1985, with more centers operating, there was more communication. There were rumors about a few male center personnel acting inappropriately with women clients, and that some places were not being properly maintained. This was a topic at an F.T.A. Board meeting. John Lilly said, with his usual simplicity, "Oh, these are problems that are easy to take care of. Create a set of guidelines, publish the guidelines in *Floating* magazine, and start to accredit centers." (You can find more information about this in the Appendix.) Due to staffing problems the accreditations did not happen.

By late 1984, bath houses in San Francisco started closing due to the AIDS scare. When Rock Hudson died of AIDS-related complications in October 1985, people were ignorant about AIDS transmission and some people started to avoid public water facilities. Since many of our sales were to commercial float centers, we were strongly affected. Business has its rules. Several months we worried about paying the rent, and some magical thing would always come through.

Nonetheless, we were confident we could increase revenue if we had a tank that was less expensive to manufacture and addressed people's objection to the amount of space the tank required. We came up with the idea of a floatation tank that could do double duty as a couch and bed. When the top was down it was a couch; to get inside and float the top was raised at an angle. When we were in production on that tank John Lilly appeared at the factory without warning and was immediately drawn to this unusual new attraction. He examined it carefully and asked some questions. The usually reserved John was wearing a big smile which made us very happy. They sold quickly.

We continually made changes to refine the design. For example, originally we used a submersible filtration system, with a magnetic drive pump, stored outside the tank. The tank owner would set it inside, close the door on the cord, and filter for a couple of hours. When the manufacturer discontinued that pump, we had to go to an external filtration system, with hoses into and out of the tank, since there were no manufacturers of a comparable submersible pump. Over time, various necessary structural refinements continued to increase the production costs until we were way above our planned budget and the price of the tank became about the same as our commercial tank, the Samadhi Classic. Unfortunately, there just was

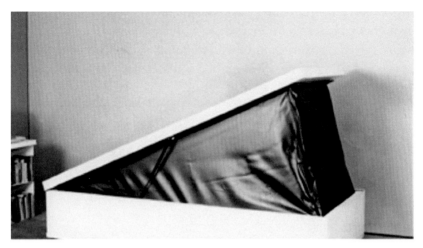

Float Furniture - from couch (top left p.132) to floation tank, above

Accountant's tank with daughter's bed over it

not enough of a market for us to be selling both. We discontinued the float furniture.

By May of 1987 the last gay bathhouse closed in San Francisco. By 1989, the number of float centers in the U.S. had decreased from more than 100 in the early part of the decade to less than fifty. With the effect of AIDS on the industry, and the financial difficulty we were having, we were uncertain whether we would continue in the business. In 1986 we had begun looking at alternatives, and we moved to Northern California in 1989. We made thirteen tank bodies to take with us. We thought this would hold us until we figured out our next steps.

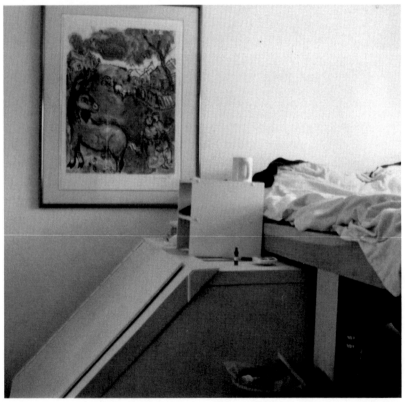

Samadhi Classic with bed on top

CHAPTER THIRTEEN

ENTERING ANOTHER WORLD
MOVING TO GRASS VALLEY,
GLENN'S HEALTH
AND E.J. GOLD

E.J. Gold teaching art

E.J. Gold

Lee

Glenn really did not like living in the city! Traffic, crowds, waiting in lines, noise, smog, freeways, honking horns, rude people…I could see that when we left the city for a short while his big smile got lots of practice. Fortunately, our Echo Park house, on a large lot, gave us an opportunity to be with nature and grow a small garden. Glenn is a country person. He needed space to raise bees, grow his own food, and breathe good air.

Where to move? Speaking with John Lilly, he suggested that one of his friends, E.J. Gold, "Sufi, transit guide and explorer of inner domains," might entertain our joining his community. John thought we might find a source of helpers there, and he was eager to support Samadhi Tank Company's success. Coincidentally, many of the people who had come to float in our Beverly Hills center had brought stories about E.J. Gold, so we were already familiar with him, by reputation.

It was a good match. From the website, the group, "The Institute for the Development of the Harmonious Human Being" is dedicated to the enablement of conscious living and dying, personal transformation, the attainment of higher personal, organizational and planetary consciousness, and service to the vision of a living universe. IDHHB works with individuals and organizations seeking tools to be of service in these areas, to expand their perceptions and awareness, and to cultivate high attention and presence."

While still in L.A. we listened to many E.J. Gold lectures and studied his work. This school was different from our schooling with Dr. Lilly where the teaching was reached through individual study of his books and direct work with him on specific projects, such as our work with the tanks. We were trying to understand the nature of this, a spiritual school. E.J. Gold was the teacher. He gave many talks that allowed an increased understanding of the principles. Later, as members of the school, we shared housing and followed protocols regarding life-cycle events and the kitchen as a spiritual setting.

During this time, I received a call from my mother, Ann, who lived in NYC, telling me her very sick sister had moved in with her, and maybe I was coming soon? I left at the speed of a daughter taking care of the important stuff. I found my sick mother caring for her younger sister. Once I arrived my mother deteriorated quickly. Perhaps my arrival allowed her to let go. I took Ann to her cardiologist. He asked her who brought her, and she told him I, Lee, worked there in his office. I began to understand that now I was in charge of my mother's health, right then, after living a continent apart for over thirty years. As her only child, it was her and me, and she was not connected to current time. Her sister also needed full time care, which I arranged with my cousins, her children. It was a very large piece of family business to be completed within a few days.

I brought my mother back to L.A. During that following year she did not recognize me, and she had some good stories about her daughter. She was mainly quiet, interior in thought. She had left the universe I was in.

As Glenn and I became uncertain about the Samadhi business in general and our life in Los Angeles in particular, our employees, seeing that we were winding down, chose to move on. In the factory, I worked on admin and sales. Glenn made the tanks to take with us to satisfy orders while we determined what we were going to do. The work required spray contact adhesive. The area was not properly ventilated, and Glenn did not otherwise protect himself from the toxicity. Before the end of the year he was experiencing hemorrhoids and extreme tiredness and started seeing a health practitioner.

At home, Ann liked wearing lipstick and always had a tube in her pocket. Now she would put lipstick on her eyebrows. Over the course of her life, how many times must she have pulled that lipstick out of her bag and run it across her lips. She had become completely interior. She seemed to have everything she needed. She smiled a lot to herself. She did not talk. She often sat facing the television, with no apparent response. Maybe the way to describe it is she was looking in its general direction and not seeing it. She was sweet and kind. I did not need anything from her. I could see she was dying, and that was okay.

In 1989 we made our move to Grass Valley, a town with a substantial artist population, a good climate for growing food, good transportation for our business, and good movie theaters. Neither too big nor too small, it was surprisingly just right! We brought Ann with us although we had no way to determine if this was okay with her. She neither objected nor agreed to going when we spoke about it. She was comfortable in the back seat of the car. On our way we stayed in a motel. All was fine. In the morning my mother announced she would not continue on with us. We called The Institute to let them know we would still be arriving that day although Ann was resisting. Claude answered the phone and spoke with Ann for a while. Claude told her he was going to have her speak with E.J. Gold. She was okay with this, and. E.J. got on the phone for at least one sentence, maybe two. At the end of their very short conversation she told us she changed her mind, that she was coming. We never found out what he told her.

Glenn

In Grass Valley, as we started to settle in, people called about buying their own tank. This was encouraging since we needed to support ourselves, and we had our thirteen tanks to sell with basically no overhead aside from assembly of the peripherals, which included the filtration and temperature control systems that required minimal space and labor. Ironically, with our limited inventory Lee tried to discourage sales, afraid we would run out. Nothing like the fear of scarcity to move sales. What could we do? Thinking long-term, without the overhead of a factory we could easily stay in business, and income from the existing thirteen could pay for new molds. In our previous tank, both sides of the flat parts (walls, top and bottom) were glued to the foam insulation. My idea was to design new molds to vacuum form the inside and outside parts, so the insulation could be inserted into a pocket that required sealing only around its perimeter. This made labor more economical by reducing the skill required and reducing the production time by seventy percent. We called Don, the owner of the company that made our vacuum formed parts, and asked if he would be willing to produce the body of the tank if I redesigned it so it only required a small amount of unskilled labor. He thought about it and two days later he said yes.

I immediately started doing my favorite thing: designing.

139

Ann lived with us for about four months before she passed. We were with her one evening. We wondered if she was still breathing. We checked her wrists. They were quiet. It seemed she had gone. It was so simple. How were we so mellow through this? I wondered if it had to do with floating.

Don, the vacuum former, made the twelve required molds and we drove back to L.A. to check the first vacuum formed pieces and to discuss how to turn them into the back, front and top, and so on.

In 1990, a year after moving to Grass Valley, we moved into a house with some other people from the Institute community. The ground floor was a common living area and kitchen. We took the large basement for ourselves as our private living area, where we also had our office. Almost immediately I started having even more severe symptoms. I could hardly walk, I was in a state of exhaustion much of the time, and it was hard to remember things. This was a difficult time. I rarely had enough energy to do the work and projects that give me satisfaction. For the first two years, I had no idea what the problem was. Then we discovered we were sleeping on moldy carpeting.

During that time, I started tracking my mental, emotional and physical energy. Any time I felt different than usual, I would go back through the previous twenty-four hours and look for a cause; a practice I continue to this day. For example, I discovered sweets would make me irritable. I noticed that others were also affected by sweets; for some it was sadness, others depression, still others anxiety. Observing the effects of my diet resulted in me cleaning it up significantly and turned me into a crusader. Clearly we needed to move. We had a hard time finding a new place that was not toxic since I had become very environmentally sensitive. Modern houses have many toxic attributes, particularly outgassing from many adhesives, most carpeting, and pressed wood.

In 1995 our friend, Claudio Naranjo, who traveled around the world giving workshops, was looking to buy a home base which would include a safe place for his book collection. We decided to combine forces. We immediately found a thirty-five-acre property that was divine. He loved it, too. Just before we signed the papers he called to tell us he could not go through with the purchase.

How could we afford this perfect solution it had taken us so long to find? Lee put out a request to our new community for people interested in buying the property with us. Many of the people in the community were artists, and this property had a twenty-four by one hundred eighty foot chicken coop, with no evidence of chickens ever having lived there, that could be used for artist studios and storage and whatever else might come up. Wonderful for Samadhi Tank Company; we used part of the chicken coop for production which has kept our overhead low, keeping the price of our tanks low. By the end of several meetings, we had eight members who were interested. We had found our new home where we have been living ever since. My health improved greatly over the next few years.

In that same time period we heard that Timothy Leary was very sick. John called us late one morning to say, "Tim Leary is in a lot of pain and you should bring a tank down for him. He is not going to be around much longer."

We were honored to be asked and were able to pack up the tank and leave for Beverly Hills in the early hours of the next morning. After a ten-hour drive, we delivered and set up the tank that afternoon.

When we arrived at Timothy's house, he and John Lilly were talking. We said hello and went about our business of unloading

Lee and Tim

141

and setting up the tank in Tim's bedroom. We were in the giving lane. We were together with two of our heroes, the ones who knew and told us what they knew. We left the tank for Tim's use. He was not around much longer.

John Lilly sent us two notes: First, "It may save Timothy's life. You're the most dedicated people I've ever met. I never saw such a good example of teamwork as I saw yesterday." And a little later, "That was the most compassionate thing I have seen from a group of people. It validated all those years inventing and experimenting with the tank worthwhile. Now I can die in peace."

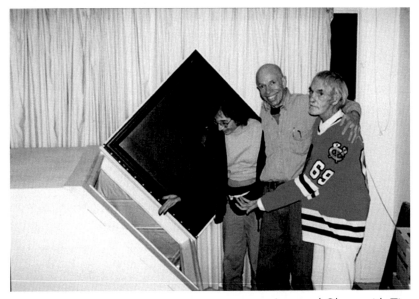

Lee and Glenn with Tim

By this time we had twelve new molds and made a run of thirty tanks. They were selling, and we were doing well. We would phone the customer's address to Don, and he would ship the tank, and we would ship the equipment pack from Grass Valley. We took one to put in our bedroom (it is still being used there by us twenty-four years later), sold eight others and had three unfulfilled orders in. The next order needed to go out and we could not reach Don.

He called a couple of days later. A sixteen-year-old had burned down his factory with all of our twelve molds, other tooling and twenty-one completed tanks. Neither of us had insurance for our property in the factory. We had to send out three tanks and had no way to do it. Basically, all of our assets had just gone up in smoke.

We found out why living in a community is so great. A new friend sent us in the direction of a small local company owned by Gabriel, a talented trade show booth designer knowledgeable in the presentation of product display. To our good luck, Gabriel was happy we had called him with our problem. He had always wanted to have a tank of his own to float in, and here we were, the founders of the first floatation tank manufacturing company. It was 1996 when he and I sat down together and discussed what was needed to provide Samadhi with tanks. We had neither the capital, vacuum former, mold maker, or time to produce molds to replace what had been lost. We needed a tank that could be fabricated quickly and easily with few molds. With Gabriel's help, we were able to deliver the outstanding orders in three months.

Health Setback

In 2001, four of us in the Samadhi Tank Company were installing two of our tanks in a recently remodeled hotel in Oakland, California. The installation took two days and all four of us were feeling very strange, with nausea, dizziness and jitters at the end of each day. A week later I was flat in bed with a very painful hemorrhoid. No one else in the group had any ongoing symptoms. My sensitivity was probably due to a weakened immune system from the two prior health challenges: the contact adhesive and the moldy carpeting. It took me a week to recover from that acute attack.

Alarming symptoms appeared on the right side of my body shortly after that. I no longer could use my right leg and was just dragging it along. I could hardly sign my name. It became a big scribble. I lost much of my intelligence and my memory. Now I had a serious problem. I needed to get some exceptional medical help. I trust the pharmaceutical industry to do what it is designed to do, to make money.

I began researching alternative health strategies and learned of the Weston Price diet on the Weston Price Foundation website, started by Sally Fallon Morell, assisted by Thomas Cowan, MD.

Dr. Price, a dentist, wrote *Nutrition and Physical Degeneration* in 1939 about his ten-year travels around the earth researching the traditional diets of primitive peoples who all had "beautiful straight teeth, freedom from decay, good physiques, resistance to disease and fine characters." Their foods were nutrient dense and supplied many times the nutrients of our foods today. The Weston Price Foundation published a quarterly journal for which Dr. Cowan wrote a recurring article. I found him to be a very knowledgeable and trustworthy medical practitioner.

It took me two years to finally find a doctor I could trust. In addition to being a founding member of the Weston A. Price Foundation, Dr. Cowan was a member of the Association for Anthroposophical Medicine, a medical system invented by the teacher and mystic, Rudolf Steiner. Dr. Thomas Cowan interviewed me for a long time, including asking me what I thought. This was the first time a doctor actually wanted to know anything about me besides my height, weight, blood pressure and medical history. At the end he said I had organophosphate poisoning.

At the time I did not connect these problems with the tank installation, but upon reflection I realized that was how I had acquired the problem. In connection with the remodel, they very well must have sprayed pesticides as part of the process. Dr. Cowan put me on the Weston Price diet and gave me several supplements. Most pesticides were made of organophosphates in 2001. They are nerve toxins designed to disrupt the nervous system of bugs. They sure disrupted mine.

More F.T.A.

Beginning in 2014 the F.T.A. and other members of the float community did their best to take leadership in an initiative by public health agencies and departments to regulate the floatation tank industry. A major issue championed by F.T.A., directed by Shoshana Leibner, was getting the agencies and departments to understand that chlorine and bromine were inappropriate water sanitizers. As a group, we were successful in convincing the Centers for Disease Control and Prevention (CDC) that the combination of ultra violet

(UV) and ozone, or UV and hydrogen peroxide (HP), were perfectly acceptable, and safer sanitizers in the floatation environment.

Shoshana Leibner also engaged the interest of Jason McDonald, Public Health Inspector in British Columbia, Canada, in finding common ground between the various interested parties. As Mr. McDonald states:

"Health officials, myself included, can do better than feeling like we are best protecting public health by having floatation conform to existing swimming pool standards. We have to see and believe in floatation as a non-drug approach to improving the physical and psychological well-being of the public. I personally feel that if one person who needs floatation misses their opportunity, it eventually leads to an increased burden of some kind to the health care system. Miscasting floatation as risky can stifle the industry and unnecessarily close tanks and businesses. By working together, the floatation industry and health officials can continue to develop appropriate minimum standards and observe more and more of the safe outcomes we currently see across North America."

Through Jason McDonald's experience floating, and his position as a Provincial Public Health Inspector, he delivers an essential and provocative point by point examination of the differences between floatation tank and public recreational water use, in our Appendix.

Back to My Health

In retrospect, Dr. Cowan's dietary approach to health satisfied the point of view I had adopted as a kid. Growing up on a farm, I knew that animals were healthiest when given the healthiest food. Having read a lot on growing the healthiest food, I knew that our produce was becoming lacking in nutrients because agriculture has depleted our topsoils. In fact, at the current rate, there is only enough topsoil for sixty more years of food production. Then we will be out of farmland. Since I knew the poor quality of even most organic food, I started increasing the amount and kind of food I was growing in our garden. We started raising chickens, ducks and geese. I did

145

whatever I could to feed them as well as I fed myself, growing what they needed to thrive. Life begets life. That is, if I want to be the most alive, I eat the most alive food, not packaged "food."

In 2015 I found a Biodynamic farming consultant, Hugh Lovel, with whom I was very simpatico. He had read John Lilly, he loved floating, and he thought diet was very important, with the health of the soil critical. He helped us move our soil into a healthier state with the right balance of all the many minerals. He said, when the soil is in balance the food reveals it through its amazingly delicious flavor.

I had worked hard to recover from pneumonia as a two-year-old and now was equally dedicated to surviving. I was a puritan on my diet. Slowly, over fifteen years, I made improvements. Dr. Cowan said most people who had what I had would have been dead by then, and only by religiously following the diet was I still alive. As I got healthier, I noticed different things affected my ability to think.

Glenn ready for work in their biodynamic garden

146

If I ate many grains I could not think or walk well or be creative. To this day, everything I consume affects my nervous system. Through my experience I have learned to be responsible; to care for my body and my mind.

I have not cared that I got poisoned or got the other health challenges. It has not been a hardship. Instead it was a blessing. I started eating a very healthy diet and raising animals and growing very healthy food. I think I am far healthier than most people my age. I have learned a lot about corporations and their agendas that go unnoticed by most people. I learned a lot about how the world works. I feel everything that happens is for a reason. It may look negative without seeing the total perspective.

How Do I Harvest That Ear Of Corn?

Runner Beans, Echinacea, Chicory

Ducks

This reminds me of my favorite Zen story. A farmer's horse ran away and the villagers said, "That's awful." The farmer said, "Maybe." The horse returned bringing with it a wild horse. The villagers said, "That's wonderful." The farmer said, "Maybe." The farmer's son, trying to tame the wild horse, was thrown and broke his leg. The villagers said, "That's awful." The farmer said, "Maybe." Military officers came through the village to conscript young men into the war and could not take the son. The villagers said, "That's wonderful." The farmer said, "Maybe."

Long Beans

Lee and Glenn in wedding attire in front of Samadhi tank

God is in a float tank right now

...and we are
just figments of
his imagination.

Early gift from Lyle Tuttle

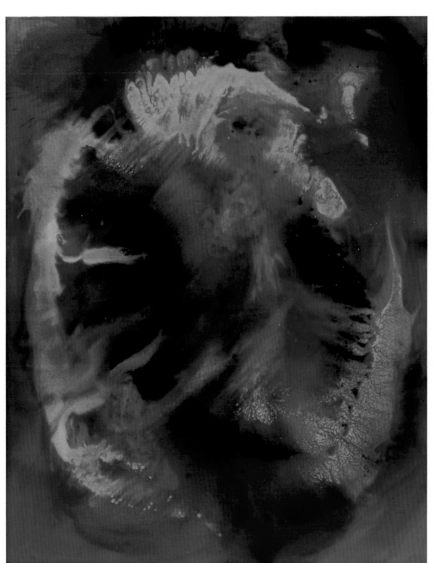

*Deep **Self*** by Lil McGill

Fetus floating in womb, Mother floating in Samadhi tank, Tank floating in ocean

San Francisco Center after-float area

Cami's twins: Asa Gabriel and Navah

CHAPTER FOURTEEN

TANK DESIGN
CREATING A DISTRACTION FREE ENVIRONMENT

Lilly Pond

Lifting Top To Float

Closing Door & Floating

Design Difficulty Required Postponing Project

Preface

The purpose of this chapter is to share the thinking process that resulted in the design of our tank, with some technical details on how we achieved some of the features. In making this a stand-alone document there is some unavoidable duplication with other places in the book. We have done our best, in that instance, to add some other dimensions to the presentation.

In our chapter on fears we mention that Dr. Lilly requested that we prepare everyone to deal with a panic attack while floating, prompted by his wife's bursting out of the tank. It could happen to anyone. Also, it is most important to make sure everyone knows to use the tank in a way that is comfortable for them.

It is important to understand how our senses operate in the floating environment. When we are still, our body slightly heats the surrounding solution. In order to remove all experience of temperature we have to remain still until that has happened. In the tank our body lies at the intersection of liquid below and air above. If the temperature is comfortable and we wait a number of minutes until we are able to let go of that intersection, what we are floating in and what is above us is experienced as one and the same.

When there are no distractions we can let go of our body and become just a point, a point of consciousness, to be, to do, to go anywhere. When there are distractions we are tied to the here and now, the reality we all know. In order to remove all distractions, we have to remove our experience of gravity, light, outside sources of sound, and temperature.

Size

Most people who are afraid are afraid of something other than claustrophobia. Therefore, we see no reason to make the tank the height of a room. To eliminate one important distraction, the floater should not notice any difference between the temperature of the solution and the air above. A taller design increases volume which would make it harder to get the air and solution temperature to feel identical. Some people feel that ping-ponging is the major distraction to address and think it can be solved with a large tank. Our tests show that a larger tank results in slightly more ping-ponging, not less. Instead, carefully lying down to float and holding a spread-eagle position for a brief twenty to thirty seconds upon entry totally handles the problem.

The human population is distributed over a wide range of sizes. For example, some men are taller than ninety-nine percent of the rest of males. Reviewing the published measurements for different percentiles of Americans, I discovered that ninety-nine percent of men are shorter than seventy-five and one-half inches. When we had our Beverly Hills center several pro basketball players came to float and found the tank size to be fine. Also at that time, we sold a tank to Michael Crichton who was more than five inches taller than ninety-nine percent of men at six feet nine inches. By the way, Michael Jordan and Scottie Pippen are six feet six inches and six feet eight inches, respectively. Our tank internal height is thirty-nine and one-half inches so most people can sit up straight inside, the length is eighty-nine and one-third inches so most can straighten their arm but not their hand and foot, and the width is forty and a half inches so most can spread their elbows. Some people would like to be able to spread their arms but most do not float that way. To accommodate this rare request the internal width would have needed to be almost double. This would have significantly increased the price of the tank and required a lot more space in center rooms and rooms at home, severely limiting the number of people able to fit it into their spaces.

Another aspect of size is our belief that all tank requirements, such as insulation, should be built into the tank rather than the room in which the tank sits. The savings in time and materials are considerable. It is a lot easier to properly waterproof a small tank than a large room. At this scale, a smaller project often presents fewer problems with better results.

Glenn - Distractions

I decided to make tanks after going to John Lilly's first workshop, and I had to learn more about removing all distractions: sound, light, temperature. For sound, I talked with a UCLA physics professor. I learned that what works to absorb sound is soft unflat materials that prevent the sound from bouncing back, and what works as a barrier to sound passing through one space or material to another is the interface of two mismatched materials where the ratio of the density of one material over the speed of sound through that material is different from the ratio of the density of the other material over the speed of sound in that material. So, if there is structure-borne sound or vibration that could come up through the bottom of the tank, then some four-inch square small pads of five layers of mismatched materials placed under the tank will significantly reduce the problem. To determine if there will be a problem you can place an ear against any wall near where the tank will go, while the problem sound is happening, and cover the other ear. What you hear will be just slightly less than what you will hear when you are in the tank.

Airborne sound is a different problem. Getting your ears under the solution surface and closing the door of the room handles airborne sound. This implies the tank is enclosed and that there are no air vents, etc., where sound can enter. To understand this issue imagine there is someone talking outside your front door. You may be able to hear a murmur, but when you open the door even a tiny crack they are easy to hear well. Nothing needs to be done to the walls of the tank room when the tank is enclosed because that provides the necessary two solid walls between the sound and the floater. Our Beverly Hills center did double duty as a working float space and promotional model. The wall between two of the tank rooms was a simple set of one-layer thick plywood sheets that could be lifted out to take photos. In the case of an open float vessel, in order to have two sets of mismatched materials the two sides of the room walls have to be decoupled from each other to create two solid walls between a sound and the person floating. Decoupled means mechanically separating the two sides of the room wall so sound does not pass through. They must also be insulated and totally waterproof. What a job! And with an open vessel, it is incredibly difficult to get the temperature of the air and water to be so similar that there is no distraction.

To make the tank light-proof is also important. If it is not, the room the tank is in must do that work. In centers that may not be difficult, but with a personal tank it is not always easy to achieve an aesthetic solution.

Opaque materials, which generally have to be black, have to be used for the tank enclosure. Tongue-and-groove must be used around the door, with dark matte surfaces. There can never be a latch or catch to keep or hold the door closed. To keep light from entering through the filtration system plumbing requires opaque materials. To keep light from entering air vents requires channels with matte surfaces and multiple turns.

The air entrance and exit must be on the same end where the floater has their head. If the air entrance is on a different end from the exit, then a lot more air flow is necessary and the air flow above the solution will be noticeable as will the difference in temperature, both of which will be distractions.

Condensation on the top is a problem in all tanks. It is easiest to understand by considering an ice-cold glass of liquid in the summer. In a humid environment, the humid air around the glass cools down. Cold air cannot hold as much moisture as warm air so some of it condenses, that is, it goes into the liquid state from the gaseous state, resulting in droplets of moisture on the outside of the glass. Since the top of the tank is always cooler than the 100% humid air in the tank, the moisture in the air right under the top condenses. Could the top be sloped so the drips would slide down the surface

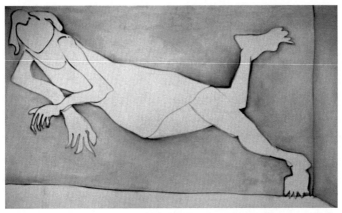

Wee Slip of a Girl by E.J. Gold

to the edge rather than falling? Our experiments suggested that a surface needed to be forty degrees or more (depending upon the material) so that condensation will slide down the surface to the edge. Even the apex of a pyramid will collect condensation droplets. To solve this issue, since 1991 we have heated the top to remove the condensation.

When John gave me the information he knew about how to make an isolation tank, one of the points he stressed was that the temperature controller needed to be very accurate. Since he was a single person floating there was information he was lacking which came out when Lee and I both floated in the same tank at different times. We found she likes the tank at one temperature and I like it .75°F (.42°C) cooler. We put the temperature halfway between. Shockingly, neither one of us was really comfortable. At that temperature she was cold, and I thought the tank was stuffy. In a public situation you might not notice if it was only that much too cold, but I do think if it was that much too hot you would notice the stuffiness.

People cannot imagine that the body needs the temperature accurate to .25°F (.21°C) because, normally, in a low humidity environment, evaporation provides for a wide comfort range. Evaporation cannot help cool the body when totally submerged, or in a tank where the lower half of the body is submerged and the upper body is in one hundred percent humidity. Since the body cannot control the temperature for itself in that high humidity environment, to be comfortable the tank must do all the work.

We realized we could use the heater in the top of the tank to both prevent condensation and to allow everyone to float at a temperature comfortable for them. People who like it cool could float with the top heater off and people who like it warmer could float with the top heater on. The warm top radiates warmth, warming the floater's skin like an infrared light in a bathroom or the sun on a cool spring morning. To work properly requires the solution temperature to be an exact exact 93.2°F (34.0°C). To adjust the solution temperature for this situation we send a thermometer calibrated to the U.S. standard because most temperature controllers and thermometers, even the oral ones, are not accurate enough.

When we started our business (and the industry) in 1972, we tried to make the tanks as inexpensive as we could. After ten to fifteen years, we began getting calls from owners wondering what to do about a part that was no longer working well. I sometimes did not have a good answer, but I knew that we wanted to ultimately build tanks that were highly durable and as reliable as possible. Our environmental impact concerns have also driven our continued interest in durability and limiting waste, both in our products and our purchases. [See the piece on the hockey stick graph in the Epilogue.] We take our responsibility as stewards of our planet seriously.

Over the years we continually made improvements and innovations to our Classic tank. In order, these included:

1. We increased the size of the air flow.
2. We moved from a small low-flow magnetic drive pump to a much larger high-flow pool and spa pump.
3. Originally the tank walls were plastic with an insulating Styrofoam sheet and a liner holding the solution. We inserted an additional plastic sheet between the Styrofoam and the liner so the foam would not get compacted over years of use.
4. We added sound isolators as an option, to prevent sound or vibration from transferring from the building structure up through the bottom of the tank.
5. We changed the thermoplastic used from less expensive more brittle styrene to ABS, a more durable plastic.
6. We further increased the air flow to eliminate the fan in the air circulation system.
7. We added a heater to the inside plastic top section to eliminate condensation.
8. We increased the temperature controller accuracy to .25°F (.14°C) from .75°F (.42°C).
9. We added internal controls to allow people to adjust the top heater from inside the tank, enabling them to have a perfectly comfortable float temperature without stuffiness. Luckily for the floating world, in order to satisfy two float perfectionists (Glenn and Lee of course), I had to design an adjustable, highly accurate temperature control system.

10. We added an ozonator for commercial installations.
11. We moved away from a pool and spa pump with a seal that could leak to a large magnetic drive pump that cannot.
12. We removed the ozonator and added an ultraviolet device.

Samadhi continues to design and offer what is widely considered the best, most distraction-free tanks on the market for personal and commercial use.

You can reach Samadhi on our website: samadhitank.com.

Painting on the shower wall tile

In the shower

CHAPTER FIFTEEN
FLOATING 2020
WHERE ARE WE NOW?

Lee at Tank factory

1.Open 2. Assemble 3. Float!

We have spent the last fifty years exploring, developing and evangelizing the benefits of floating. This has been our life's work and we are grateful for, and humbled by, the many friends we have made along the way, and those who have benefitted from our lifelong passion.

Most inspiring is the increasing awareness of the enormous benefits of floating. There is growing enthusiasm for floating as a tool to relieve the stresses and strains of our always-on, always-connected world. Floaters are able to turn down the noise, reset and re-center themselves and flourish despite the incessant demands on their time and attention. They can be calm, be creative, be productive, or simply Be irrespective of whatever is happening.

Thousands of people have shared with us the direct benefits they enjoy from floating. Floating has also been enthusiastically supported in the public sphere. In print, interviews and, more recently, even in television commercials, testimonies abound regarding the ways floating contributes to wellbeing and performance. [Please note: these testimonials are not intended to convey any implicit or explicit endorsement of Samadhi Tank Company.]

In the sports world, numerous athletes have cited the positive impacts of floating. Steph Curry, National Basketball Association Most Valuable Player in 2014 and 2015, reports, in *Business Insider, Feb. 4, 2016*, that floating clears his head allowing for "improved focus and perspective." He goes on to say that the benefits from floating continue to increase over time.

Bill Belichick, Head Coach for the New England Patriots, learned about floating from a visit with the U.S. Special Forces. The Patriots introduced floating to their players in 2014. In a Nov. 2, 2019 NBC Sports feature, team members reported both strong physical and mental stress relief. In the *Feb. 1, 2019 Sports Illustrated*, Bill Belichick reported that Tom Brady gets so much benefit from floating that he has a personal tank in his home. Aly Raisman, U.S. Women's Gymnastics World and Olympic Gold Medal Winner, also floats. In *Bustle, July 9, 2016*, she credits the tank with providing that "crucial" place to really rest.

Mindfulness and meditation, which in the 1970s were discounted by many for being New Age mumbo jumbo, have become far more accepted (and promoted) by those who have become practitioners. Ray Dalio, founder of the world's largest hedge fund, Bridgewater Associates, evangelizes about the benefits of Transcendental Meditation, calling it "the single biggest influence" in his life.

Dalio does not connect floating to his meditation practice, but many others have. Deanna DeBara, writing in a Feb 5, 2018 article in *Men's Health Magazine*, gives a strong endorsement of how floating increases the benefits of meditation. After reading the testimonials of Steph Curry and Joe Rogan, as a meditator and yogi, and someone who writes about health, she had to try it. Floating gave her the experience of genuine relaxation she had been searching for, and the ability, in just thirty minutes, to access a deep calm only read about in meditation books. As many others also report, it was like meditating on steroids. Her transformative experience left her dreaming of her next float opportunity.

The Medical community has also weighed in. Voluminous anecdotal evidence indicates reduced stress and anxiety, muscle relief and an increased ability to focus along with a generally improved sense of well-being among floaters. Neuropsychologists report that through floating many can now achieve those sorts of deep meditative states in an environment that does not require medication.

The U.S. Navy has taken notice. Navy Seals have been using floatation tanks to increase rates of learning new languages, with reductions in time-to-fluency from six months to six to eight weeks, made possible by the receptivity and internal noise reduction floating provides. Additionally, Seals have used floatation tanks to treat concussive injuries including TBI (traumatic brain injury) with noticeable improvement. In one case a Seal who had experienced constant headaches for more than two years experienced immediate relief after his first float.

In another remarkable example of how floating might be of use in helping deal with the impacts of war, Michael Harding, a 23-year-old Australian soldier stationed in Afghanistan, was medically discharged from the army in 2012 with severe PTSD after his second-in-command was shot and killed in combat. He suffered from insomnia with nightmares and night sweats. To deal with these symptoms, Harding tried therapy and took multiple medications. He turned to yoga, juicing, meditation, and medicinal marijuana with little relief. These helped somewhat but the anxiety and muscle spasms continued. Then floating was recommended. As reported in Float Hopes: The Strange New Science of Floating (Time.com, 2020), he was skeptical at first, but he "really mellowed out" after floating. It opened him to experience a "more confident, comfortable headspace."

The blogosphere is another place we have seen evidence of the ways floating can be beneficial. An anonymous coder on Reddit shared (all emphasis is as posted):

So, to preface, I'm an engineer, I'm pretty high strung (stress, organizing - think typical engineer) so facts and logic play a pretty big role in my thinking. I'm not very crunchy granola. I mentioned to my wife I like to try weird stuff like this, so she bought me a session for Christmas.

I also take LOTS of sleep aids. Melatonin, Tylenol PM and others - if I'm lucky I can get to sleep in under an hour most nights.

I went, I floated, I have a bad back, it was Ok. I enjoyed it. I dozed, I had some dreams, I phased in and out. It was cool, it wasn't mind altering, it wasn't life changing, it was good.

NOW: The weird part. I come out thinking, "That was ok, I'll try it again." I'm pretty relaxed even for me. I get home, I hug my family, I sit on the couch and I sink down into a relaxed state I have not felt in YEARS. It lowered my floor for the ability to relax WAY WAY down there. The relaxed where you sink into the couch and you do not give a shit about anything. Life is great, and then I immediately fell asleep sitting on the couch. "Damn I must have been relaxed, maybe I'll just go lay down in bed." I fell asleep in...I would estimate under 3 minutes. That does not happen to me. Ever... It continued like this for 3-4 weeks.

Going Global

Hundreds of floatation tank centers around the world host thousands of floaters every week. We have shipped tanks to residential and commercial locations across the United States and Canada, South America, Europe and the Middle East, Russia, the Far East and Australia. And, we have been joined in our efforts to make floating available by numerous other tank manufacturers. We still believe Samadhi products provide the best floating experience in the world, but we love the fact floating is becoming more and more available and people are integrating floating into their lives.

SECTION TWO

THIS SECTION INCLUDES WRITINGS BY US AND OTHERS TO GIVE A SLICE OF THE BREADTH OF EXPERIENCES FOUND IN THE TANK.

WHY FLOAT?
OUR APPROACH

Lee

Why Float? This is the hardest easy thing I had to write. How am I going to explain it? It is when everything is as it should be. I know that no extra anything is needed for everything to be as it wants to be. I am being Lee. My steps are going in the right direction without any thinking, and when I happen to think about it I am often smiling.

The world is simple, it is right, it is easy, it is as it should be. I think it has to do with floating, or floating has to do with it! I float every morning for about an hour and have been doing that for at least 45 years. My joke is that I am well marinated; and it may be just as simple as that! Spending time in the tank makes changes in my mind and body. A quietness comes from the empty space, and along with the quiet comes an appreciation of simply being where I am. It is not easy to describe since, at those moments, it is as if there is not anything to describe. What is coming into my vision seems as if it is just what is there, without labels or reasons.

Sometimes, I lie in the tank and rerun segments of my life. I have seen myself act in precisely the same way, over and over again, especially in significant scenes; the same scenario over and over and over again. It can continue to be serious and significant until, after numerous reruns, I invariably start laughing at my own behavior. I can be lying in the tank with nothing going on, and suddenly I start laughing that I have actually considered these things to be so important. In the tank, they all seem like a great joke, sometimes at my own expense!

Glenn

There are many ways to use the tank and many things to use it for. The tank was invented by Dr. Lilly to research consciousness. To a significant degree I tend to think of all the ways of using the tank as being more conscious. What is consciousness? For me it is the state of being aware in the present moment.

Due to my right side still being weak from organophosphate

166

poisoning, I shuffle which results in me tripping and falling a lot. Often I break my fall to the ground by catching myself with my outstretched left arm. At one point in time I began having chronic pain in my left shoulder. In bed and in the tank it would hurt. I started putting my attention on the discomfort. I would not try to do anything with it. Whenever I fell, I had several emotions as I was lying there flat on my face, swearing. I was not only obviously upset that I had tripped yet again but also irritated I had again aggravated my shoulder and disappointed and frustrated that I had not been paying sufficient attention to walking properly by lifting my foot but was instead basically, sleep walking. These attached emotions inhibited easy healing so I moved my attention to the emotions. I waited, and they soon started to come up for me to experience. I simply experienced them as fully as I could. I went through this same scenario five days in a row until the discomfort was reduced so much that I did not bother with it anymore; it simply dissolved. This provided me a great example of using consciousness to heal.

A healer of mine told me a story. Once, while on the beach in Hawaii, his daughter, wearing low heels, stepped on his wife's bare foot. He saw a red spot develop, with another color in the center. She kept her attention on her injury, right then, and he watched while the two concentric spots gradually faded. They eventually totally disappeared along with all of the pain. All better right then. Another healer Lee and I went to years ago did the same with a very bad cut and it closed up and disappeared!

So if we put all of our attention, actually all of our consciousness, on an injury as soon as it happens, just by being with it, not trying to change it, just experiencing the pain and the emotions, simply observing them, we may be able to save ourselves a lot of later work or aggravation.

For a while I was going to a group once a week and in the group, whenever this woman talked, I felt put down, made smaller. It irritated me. I went into the tank and called on the experience of irritation that I felt whenever she spoke. After a while the irritation disappeared, and I was faced with a new hurt which I really did not want. I experienced that pushing away, that desire to not be experiencing my pain. I hung out there, anyway. Suddenly, I had this picture of my father running to the basement because of something my mother said. I did not want to deal with that at all. I felt pain seeing him suffer. While floating, I experienced the pain I had previously avoided. I just hung out there and I remembered the experience and observed my sensations, feelings and thoughts. The sensation subsided. I was relieved. In an empty tank without an agenda, things can come up to look at and clear away.

Moving so fast we generally do not pause to process it all. In the tank the volume of the mental chatter can get turned up and the most urgent gets processed. If we do that frequently enough or long enough, free of distractions, the chatter can subside enabling us to find ourselves centered in being.

I have to float or meditate every day. When I meditate, twice a day is best; my life is richer and fuller, and I am more functional. By stepping away from my life for a few moments and seeing everything from another perspective, I get increased clarity of direction. Being more aware I am more present in relationships. I see myself more objectively and accept myself and others with less criticism. Being more present, I am more aware of what is happening.

How do I take the space or consciousness I achieve in the tank with me outside the tank? The first thing I do is note what the space is. Then I feel gratitude for being in that space. The hard part is to maintain that space when in consensus reality. The other thing I do is create a trigger. Periodically, when I come out of the tank, open and at peace, I rub a spot on my body to create a trigger. After a number of repetitions, the trigger is set. When I want to get into that space I rub the spot, for example, just before going on stage to give a presentation. Eventually I can just recall the space and move into it.

I would say the best use of the tank these days for me is receiving solutions to problems. Often I do not even need to work on them anymore. By asking for the answers and intending to receive them, they often show up as I am getting out of the tank or in the shower. What used to require lots of effort in the tank years ago now happens automatically just in the process of life. I receive creative ideas effortlessly. I feel so blessed and thankful. The more I touch Spirit by leaving my mind and moving into my heart, i.e., being present, the more Spirit enters my life.

WE GENERALLY DISCOURAGE PROGRAMMING.
WE PROVIDE THESE FOR INSPIRATION.

When we, Lee, Laurie and Glenn, were editing the book we read the following stories aloud. We had each read numerous of these privately to ourselves and found them more impactful reading them aloud to each other. If convenient, you may want to try that. After reading one of them aloud, Laurie remarked that she would find it valuable to read weekly.

WE INVITE YOU TO HAVE YOUR OWN EXPERIENCES.

An Accountant's Travels to Samadhi
Gary Abreim

It was 1975 and I was volunteering in the
EST office (remember EST?) calling people
who had just completed the training to see
if they wanted to do a continuing seminar.
Glenn & Lee Perry was the next card in my
call pile and they immediately responded that
they wanted to register. There is a spot on the
card for occupation and Glenn said he was the manufacturer of
floatation tanks. "Really?" I said.

I had just read John Lilly's book *Center of the Cyclone* where I
was first introduced to the concept of floating in salt water in dark
isolation and was more than very intrigued. Glenn said that his
experience in a John Lilly workshop inspired him to start building
affordable tanks for personal use, out of cardboard no less. Glenn
had a regular job (sort of) and worked from home. He was a senior
systems designer for Scientific Data Systems which developed
revolutionary data processing technology for its time. He was a
telecommuter before that term was in the lexicon…pretty rare to
be able to work this way. I was impressed.

My excitement on the call was obvious and I got an invite to
come over to float at their house in Echo Park. Here I was this
Jewish accountant with thick glasses who was a rising star at a Big
8 CPA firm who opted out and decided that was not the world for
me. I was curious…very curious…and I wisely turned down a life
of wearing a coat and tie. A float was my next adventure and who
knew where it would lead?

A few days later I was ready for my big tank immersion and
got my float orientation from Lee. Glenn & Lee had two tanks.
Not surprising to have two tanks since this was L.A.…one of
the major centers of the new age movement…psychedelics and
all that inner explorer phenomenon stuff was going on along
with Carlos Castaneda, the Moody Blues, *2001 Space Odyssey*
& the Bodhi Tree Book Store. So why not his and her tanks?
Actually, they floated religiously every day and needed the extra

tank. They rarely missed floating. Who knew I was soon to join them?

During my float orientation Lee emphasized that I was in complete control of my experience and to most importantly keep the salt water out of my eyes. She said that there were no shoulds or bad guys in the tank. I discovered that the tank was a pretty safe place and the only bad guys were the ones I created in my mind.

When the knock on the tank came at the end of my hour I found myself disoriented and slow in returning from wherever I went. I felt like I stepped out of time and had entered a profound space in between my thoughts. When I got out everything was shimmering and I felt lighter. Talk about starting a new day…how about a new life? My experience was psychedelic without taking psychedelics.

Anyways, the tank seemed like an exciting opportunity to continue probing and turning over the stones on my path of revealing the Great Mystery. I had dabbled a bit in psychedelics and pot was enjoyable and useful, which I mixed with a variety of therapies, a dash of the Synanon game, frequent trips to the redwoods of the Santa Cruz mountains, all in my newly acquired used 1971 VW van. Ram Dass' *Be Here Now* was my guidebook.

I was a late arriver to the summer of love and Woodstock and the Grateful Dead culture; however, I had this time machine (the tank) which served me well in opening pathways. I'll have you know that I did make it to the US Festival at my daughter's encouragement and was part of the three hundred thousand to take in the great bands of the time along with the first satellite space bridge to the Soviet Union…so there. That experience was an opening to another life chapter which I'll save for another book which I may or may not write.

After my first float I realized I had to have my own tank. Glenn came over to install one in my daughter's bedroom and a bunk bed was built above it which my daughter liked. I loved floating and got it down to where I could float before work even for five minutes. I became adept at dropping into this magic space after a few minutes in the tank. Midnight to dawn floats during the period when the world quiets down were supreme.

This was an exciting time for floating. To be able to provide this experience to others and be with people after they floated was a treat in itself. I was a new age obstetrician helping deliver people to their new me. It was a rich fulfilling time in my life.

It was with Lee & Glenn that I learned about being an active listener and the importance of validating someone's personal experience. Lee and Glenn had a natural ability and found joy in doing this. They lived in a constant enthusiastic state of curiosity and wonder AND they were my dearest friends...lucky me!

Airline flight crews would come to float at the Beverly Hills center to reset their clocks from jet lag. Artists came who were dealing with creative blocks. Dancers and athletes came to work out their kinks. Most importantly the tank was the best stress reliever on the planet and I began to learn that stress relief was the key to opening and discovery. A swim in the ocean in Maui was pretty good; however, the carbon footprint was a little high. Gatherings with John Lilly, Richard Feynman, Timothy Leary and other pioneers of inner exploration made for very exciting times.

Over the years, my float world continued to unfold. It was the Big Chill experience. More recently, Shoshana, Lee's daughter and a chip off the old block, brought a tank to Burning Man! Now being without a tank at home, the float gods graced me several years ago with a float center in Sebastopol, California where I now live and float.

Forty-four years later the tank continues to be the safest place to be...no intruders...my holy temple...my playground...my art studio...my mystery space. It was in the tank that I began to appreciate my uniqueness. Being a little odd and different were qualities and something I became delighted to accept.

Thanks Lee....Thanks Glenn.

Tales of the Tank
Kathleen Ann Geisse, Ph.D.

My life changed irreparably on September
21st. First in 1988. Then again in 1990. On
September 21, 1988, in the course of a long
peaceful run on a country road, I was hit
from behind by a vehicle traveling at forty-
five mph. The car struck me in the calves, causing me to flip up
onto the hood, where I shattered the windshield with my head. I
was subsequently catapulted forward. As the road loomed before
me, I remember thinking that I had to stay on my feet, that if I
struck the pavement there would be no hope. I landed on my feet
and bounced. And bounced. And bounced again. When it was all
over, I gathered myself together, walked to the side of the road and
sat on the railing that was there. It was the last time for some time
that I was to walk without aid.

At the scene of the accident, I was called bionic woman. It
looked as if I would escape with only minor cuts and bruises. It
was, however, only a short while before I realized that I was not
OK, and in the years to follow I was to wish over and over that I
had not survived the impact.

I spent nearly two years in darkened quiet rooms. At the two-
year point, I began to feel a little better. I started to pick up the
pieces of my life. But these pieces were scattered once again on
September 21, 1990, when I was rear-ended on the freeway by a
pick-up truck with brake failure. I received another strong blow
to the head and whiplash, which was to leave me with RSD, reflex
sympathetic dystrophy, a painful debilitating syndrome in which
continuous excess sympathetic discharge from malfunctioning
nerves leads to pernicious trophic changes. There is of yet no cure,
nor even any meds to lessen the pain as conventional painkillers
have no effect.

After the first accident I was seen in the Ivory Towers, but the
extreme somatic discomfort of the second accident led me to seek
alternative help (of which I knew nothing at the time). I went to a
chiropractor, had therapeutic massage in conjunction with physical

therapy sessions, did acupuncture and biofeedback. Nothing seemed to help. In fact, my symptoms worsened. I went back to traditional medicine to devastating effect, ending up in Long Beach Memorial with an epidural infection.

I once more sought out alternative meds. Advanced alternative medicine, I suppose you could call it. I tried craniosacral therapy. I tried magnetic therapy. I did a type of torture-massage called microfiber reduction. I saw a doctor in LA who used a computer from Germany to perform a kind of high-tech kinesiology. I was Rolfed. I did macrobiotic shiatsu. I saw a Barbara Brennan healer. I tried scalp acupuncture, Chinese herbs, and homeopathics. I drank Noni juice, wheatgrass juice, took Manna aloe products, did hydrogen peroxide therapy, colored light therapy. Then I tried neuromuscular therapy. The therapy itself did not help a mite, but the therapist did. We were both kind of "tool" junkies and would often have discussions along these lines (during the short period in which I saw him, we both bought chi-gong machines and magnetic mattresses). One day he said that the one tool he really wanted was a floatation tank. I smirked. I thought he was being facetious. I had heard of floatation tanks but could not understand how simply lying in a pool of water could be of any benefit. I did not need to be cradled in a womb; I would rather swim laps. I had thought that a sense of comfort was floating's only benefit. I was obviously very wide of the mark.

Before I began floating, I used to bristle when that oft-repeated alternative practitioner mantra came at me: there are no accidents; all accidents happen for a reason. Now I feel that if those accidents were the only way I was to get into a tank, they were welcome. My first float was in April of 1995. It was only fifty minutes, but in that brief period I felt my twisted body begin to straighten itself out. In subsequent floats, as I lay in the tank, my head would whip one way, then whip the other; then my hip would move; there would be a crack down my back, a release in my neck. It was not I who was doing this or perhaps it was some more powerful I.

In the beginning, I floated several times a week for an hour and a half at a time. I felt as if I wanted to float longer and daily if I could, but the center in San Francisco was busy, and even had

174

scheduling not been a problem, long daily floats there would have been prohibitively expensive. A little sleuthing led me to a tank in Los Gatos (about an hour and fifteen-minute drive southwest of San Francisco) whose owner basically let me have free run of the tank for a very small fee. I took daily open-ended floats of five to seven hours on the long eves of summer.

I ordered my own tank in July and had it set up by August. In my own tank I was at first floating six hours daily, then as time passed five, four, and three hours. After every float, I felt a little better than I did after the float before. I am also able to stand a little straighter. As calibration, when I first started floating my right leg was one-half inch shorter than the left; they are now even. In addition, as sympathetic activity is reduced to near zero in the tank, in the window of inactivity I (empowered I) have been able to go into the RSD-affected areas to heal the original damage. I have healed enough so that other modalities do now make a difference, and I am presently doing chiropractic and some kinesiology as adjunct to speed the recovery process. "Full catastrophic healing" is now on my horizon, but this does not mean I will be giving up my quotidian three hours.

Floating is an integral part of my life. It is my daily adventure. And each float is an adventure. I had once conceived of floating as a passive activity, but it is anything but. Every float is a journey, the sum of which is a journey to the self.

Floating Yoga
Shoshana Leibner

My mother, Lee Perry, asked if I could recommend something to address a mysterious discomfort and weakness she had developed in her legs. I asked a lot of questions to get to the root of her pain. As we talked, it turned out her dis-ease was numbness and a lack of strength in her thighs, and pain in her knee. Drawing upon my background in dance and yoga, I imagined a series of stretches and muscle strengthening routines. Since Lee had been floating since the beginning of time and was very comfortable inside her Samadhi Tank, it occurred to me that the gravity reduced float environment would be ideal to work in. I had her stretch out, extend her arms above her head and lengthen from her fingertips through her toes, bringing attention to her breath. The key to this exercise was for her to feel the alignment of her spine and inner core. This was the first use of the asanas (postures) I modified for the floating environment. The first step in Lee's recovery was to practice this daily. Floating Yoga was created.

In dance I learned that body alignment is the first element of ease (the opposite of dis-ease). The first step to maintaining proper alignment is to address the feeling in the body and the tension that pulls the body away from its center. The center of human alignment is in the pelvic girdle which connects the trunk to the lower extremities. Sometimes our bodies play tricks on us. Pain felt in a part of the body other than its actual source even has two names – referred pain and radiating pain. For example, Lee was aware of the pain in her knee. Although she was not experiencing lower back pain, that was the source of the problem. Bending her knees, planting the soles of her feet on the floor of the tank, and tightening her buttocks and stomach muscles to elevate her coccyx, every day for several minutes, strengthened her lower back and thighs and her knee pain diminished.

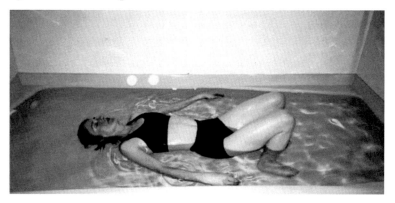

Sometimes, while floating, supported in warm salty solution, moving my body and connected with my breath, the weightlessness makes it easy to elongate and stretch and I am able to explore pure motion. I can access the individual joints freely. I often mentally scan my body for any discomfort. As I float, I release and sink deeper and connect to my core. I begin to unwind the tension in my muscles, feeling exactly where the pain originates. Floating regularly has given me the essential tools for the body awareness necessary to use this dancer's body correctly.

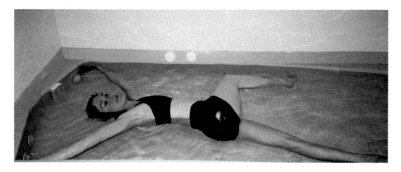

Photos courtesy of Float Dreams 2020

Float Experience
Zerin Beattie

I have been an avid floater for approximately seven years. Over the years I have floated around three hundred times, each one being remarkably different, but beautifully similar at the same time. Floating has been an incredible addition to the medicine bag of deeper discovery I have fortunately been able to build over the years. This medicine bag includes meditation, plant medicine, martial arts, floating, silent retreats, movement, world travel, discussion, and more. All of these components help me understand how my internal environment influences my external environment, and how my external environment influences my internal environments… and floating… has been one powerful piece of medicine.

In July 2018 at the beginning of a new chapter in my life, I floated for thirty days in a row and the imprint left on me still to this day (almost two years later) was unfathomable. Through the four-week span, each week my experience evolved.

Week one put me through deep relaxation and deep recovery, as if my battery was being recharged from years of neglect; thinking I was operating at one hundred percent but viscerally recognizing it was probably more around sixty-five percent. Each float during this week was allowing me to go deeper and deeper into calmness and relaxation.

Week two was the experience of discovering deep parts of my subconscious, gently flooding my awareness with tasks I was "needing" to accomplish, memories, worries, fears, providing a deeper understanding of the hidden internal fabrics that build who I am. Silence and stillness are both phenomenal medicine for helping us understand the path we are on, and there's no place that provides that like the float tank. The minimal input registered by the brain in the float tank allowed me to build a relationship with my internal world without outside influence.

Week three was fueled with an incredible surge of energy. The feeling of a fully charged battery of organic connectivity surged, creating an awakened sense of being, presence, and attunement to the world around, as well as the world within—a visceral sensation of being turned ON.

Week four provided a perspective that I have only felt during martial arts training or plant medicine ceremonies, a honed sense of harmony with potential chaos around the whole perimeter of my perception, the chaos of my new chapter. I felt the pressure around me and floating helped me stay grounded within a harmonious way of being without the pressure crumbling the system.

Each week added insightful additions to my own personal awareness of my internal world, and perhaps consciousness in general. One of the main takeaways from this experience was my perception of time. I knew I was in the float tank for sixty minutes, yet some floats felt like four minutes and some floats felt like four hours. This intriguing perspective came with me into the "real" world. I became able to hone so deep into the present moment that twenty minutes could feel like a full hour. I began to operate with more depth and presence throughout the day. Through floating I am able to feel the moment presently and deeply, and the possibilities available.

Insights On The Benefits of Floatation Therapy in Conjunction With Acupuncture. Shaitsu and Counselling

Dr. Mychelle Whitewood, doctor in
Traditional Chinese Medicine

How floatation therapy can help heal and realign the body, mind and soul through the body's own matrix that is connected to the earth and all that is.

We have seen the movie *Matrix*, watched things on YouTube, meditated and some of us have experienced firsthand things that help explain the connectedness of matter and energy; the connection that humans have to the universe. How all things on the planet and the Universe are connected and affect everything. How a single drop of water can have a rippling effect on the still water in a pond, or the flap of a butterfly wing is felt a million miles away.

As a practitioner of Traditional Chinese Medicine with over twenty-five years' study and training as my base, a passion for learning as much as I can about the healing arts to repair and help fellow humans back into health in a holistic way, it was a natural process to add floatation therapy into my practice.

Having first read about sensory deprivation in Harry Palmer's book *Living Deliberately* back in the early 90s, I was curious about the experience of being in an isolation tank, but not sure I could stay in one for hours at a time. I did not give it any more thought until a random email in 2018 invited me to float so I could refer patients. When I looked into floating another random ad popped up with a business for sale, I felt very drawn to find out more so by the end of the day I had booked myself into the float center that was up for sale. As soon as I entered the float tank I realized that this was a game changer and the next big thing to happen in healing and helping anybody and everybody to return to a better state of health, simply by doing nothing so to speak. I came out of my first float calm and relaxed like so many people do; but my mind went into overdrive about how I could bring all my worlds together and be able to afford to purchase this business, let alone run it parallel to my private practice.

While attending the Beijing Float Conference in 2018 to deliver my maiden talk, I met Shoshana Leibner and we had an immediate connection. She has been so helpful in keeping me on track with the history and research of Floatation therapy, since it was her mother Lee and stepfather Glenn Perry, who made the first floatation tanks available for the public. I do not think there is anything Shoshana does not know when it comes to the industry and the research.

My personal experience in clinical practice has been amazing and inspiring; I seem to be able to get better results with my patients, especially on the emotional level. One example that comes to mind is a woman seventy-four years of age that came in for bladder problems and was on a two hundred mg daily dose of Zoloft (antidepressant medication) for the past twenty years. Her doctor had told her that she would have to take it for the rest of her life. With weekly acupuncture and float sessions she was able to give up taking her medication after nine months.

Another gentleman, who had fractured his lumbar at work, was told he required surgery which he was against. Due to the nature of his injury, in the early weeks very little could be done in terms of physical therapies i.e. massage, chiropractic osteopathy or physiotherapy. His main source of pain relief was strong medication. He came in wanting to see if floatation could help him. After his first float he immediately lost the fluid that had built up around his waist which was from the inflammation. He reported back that he was at least able to get a full night's rest without being awakened by pain. This, on an emotional level, was also huge. To date he floats two or three times a week and has acupuncture weekly as well. The speed of his recovery has been amazing; when there is a decrease of pain in the body, healing can be much more rapid not just on a physical level, but emotionally.

It would be easy to write about the many cases that I combine with my services of acupuncture, massage, and counselling with floatation therapy, but for me it really is about the synergistic effect that happens on all levels of the body and mind that allows for a more complete system of healing in each individual.

And it is not just the use of acupuncture, any therapy can be enhanced when used with floatation therapy and I encourage others to float before or after they visit their practitioner. This can and does have a calming effect before a session. In the case before a counselling therapy session one can think about what they want to talk about and be calm going in, but also afterwards to integrate what has happened in a therapy session.

I look at it both from a Traditional Chinese medicine perspective as well as Western medicine and even the quantum realm and esoteric. Floating is a very holistic therapy, right down to the single cell that requires magnesium for photosynthesis. In our body the magnesium sulphate helps hydrate our cells and plays a vital role in removing inflammation, be that fluid and/or toxins. This aids in reducing stress; something so simple can have such cascading effects throughout our system.

From a Chinese medicine understanding, Epsom salt is bitter and salty; this has a relationship with the flavours of the Heart (FIRE element and bitter flavour) and the Kidney (WATER element and salty flavour), respectively. Bitter has a drying action and resolves damp or excess fluids; Salty is something that can soften hard masses, has a cooling and descending nature. Both working together to balance the fire and water elements of the body or the Heart and Kidney. These two elements are so important at regulating the Yin and Yang of our system.

Thank you Dr. Lilly for having the enquiring mind to question and seek out the adventure within our conscious and our subconsciousness and building the first isolation tank. And thank you to Glenn and Lee Perry for building the first floatation tank for the public to also experience floatation therapy and the many levels that it helps in the healing journey.

Thought Layers
Doug Brettin

A software engineer contacted us with a request to use our tank for a week, with the hope of floating up to three hours each day. He had never been in a tank before. For ten years he had been practicing yoga and meditation and now was drawn to the idea of experiencing an isolated environment to achieve the aim of exploring his thought processes.

Once I had read John Lilly's books *Programming and Meta-Programming the Human Bio-Computer, Center of the Cyclone,* and *The Deep Self,* I absolutely had to try floating. I had always wanted to further explore the depths of the thinking process, and perhaps experience the lowest layer of thought. You may be interested in my thought exploration which follows (in italics) or you may prefer to skip it now and return once you have read the balance of my piece.

Earlier in my life, I had a striking experience of what might be the origin of thought, and subsequently worked out a hierarchy of the intensities of thought processing, I call the layers of thought. I hoped that by isolating myself in a blank environment I could possibly experience some of the mechanics of thought that I could not sense by other methods, such as sitting meditation.

The layers could be conceived of as being like translucent or lightly colored films, each one lying on top of the next. If a person could examine a single layer, it would appear somewhat clear. However, many layers are usually operating at the same time. We normally experience a combination of all the films. It is very difficult to see through to the bottom. The aim of this series of floats was to peel back each layer to experience the lowest ones on the stack.

At each layer, the mind is working at increasing volumes, or intensities, of thinking. A thought begins deep within, and exists very softly and quietly, with low intensity. As it travels outward through the consciousness the volume increases, until it reaches the throat and mouth, where it ultimately becomes audible. As the thought materializes, it gains intensity, until it ultimately is expressed as vocal words. Of course, the topmost layer is typically called speech, rather than thought. However, this hierarchy of thought is more about the evolution of expression, so speaking is included at the top, as the most overt and forceful layer. When speaking we use the jaw, tongue, lungs, and facial muscles to make audible sounds to communicate with others. In this way, other beings can hear what one is thinking.

Just below this level, a person may have their mouth closed, and they are not speaking out loud, but the tongue may be moving slightly. Perhaps even the jaw is moving a bit. They are internally mouthing the words they are thinking. This is the stage just before opening the mouth to express something. It feels as if one is speaking the words, but keeping the mouth shut, and no sound is made. One is thinking with enough force to cause the tongue to move, and perhaps even the facial muscles to move.

The next level down, or inward, is thinking without physically articulating the words using the muscles inside one's mouth. Here one can hear their own voice inside doing the thinking. This is probably the most common level one works with while pondering things. The work on such things as thinking things through, or planning, or trying to come to an understanding happens at this level. This is considered the conscious mind, or conscious thinking.

Further down exists thought without one's voice attached. This thinking almost feels purely electric. It feels as though it is not oneself doing the thinking, but rather thought that is coming from somewhere deeper. This is what is called the voice within. It seems almost to not be oneself thinking. It also feels a bit uncontrolled. Some may call this the voice of intuition. This is the beginning of the realm of the unconscious.

Beyond this, things start to get interesting. It is almost impossible to quiet the mind, or focus enough, to sense anything below the previous, almost unconscious, level. However, something is going on there. There is a stream containing the ideas and concepts that one will soon be thinking about. It is as if while we are busy thinking on the higher levels, there is a second mind operating down here on a less controlled level. It is from here that ideas 'pop into' our mind.

Sometimes one can almost feel the idea materialize from somewhere deep inside, where there is no form to thoughts. To consistently experience thought at this level, and not entertaining the higher levels, would be to experience the "emptiness" extolled across the centuries by Zen poets. It is the realm of the Rishis, the seers of thought.

Deeper yet, memories and emotions are stored within the body in the form of groups of cells and chemical structures: neurons, peptides, and the like. These are the building blocks of future thoughts. This could be considered the absolute lowest layer, a realm in which the most primary constructs of ideas reside, before thought takes form. Somewhere between this physical molecular building block level, the physical storage level, and the realm in which thoughts begin to materialize, there is a sort of translation. At the level of translation, emotions and memories combine to become an impulse at the intuitive level.

This combining is strikingly similar to the Biblical creation story, in which the Earth was without form, and void, and darkness was upon the face of the deep. This is the state of stored memories and emotions, a formless and void lake. The spirit of God moved upon the face of the waters. The internal lake is then somehow stirred, resulting in differentiation of objects and the rise of nomenclature.

The question is, how much of this process of combining, or translating, or formulating of thoughts, can be experienced? Is it possible to dive so deeply that one can actually sense the process of the creation of thought? Such an endeavor would require shutting down all the higher levels of thought, passing through the realm of 'emptiness', and getting down to the level of pure memory and emotion, yet remaining somehow cognizant of what one is experiencing. Is it possible to dive that deeply and experience that realm without polluting the experience by thinking about it?

Once I had read John Lilly's books Programming and Meta-Programming the Human Bio-Computer, Center of the Cyclone, and The Deep Self, I absolutely had to try floating. I had always wanted to further explore the depths of the thinking process, and perhaps experience the lowest layer of thought.

The floatation tank seemed to offer an ideal environment for deep exploration. A friend had used a tank at a commercial float center and told me the experience was superficial. The staff was hurried, the tank was not dark, nor silent, and the water didn't seem to be at the right temperature. He could faintly hear people talking and music outside. I needed the real thing. John Lilly wrote that he worked closely with Samadhi Tank Company to develop the first commercial floatation tanks. I contacted them to ask if they could recommend a good place to float, a place that offered an authentic experience. To my surprise, they invited me to float at their headquarters in Grass Valley, California.

I scheduled a series of floats over a seven-day period. The first day would be a one-hour orientation float. The next five days I would float three hours each day. On the last day I would float six to eight hours to explore deeply. With nearly twenty hours of tank time over the course of seven days, I could test my hypothesis about the lowest layers of thought. Perhaps I could find other things going on among the lowest layers that would expand my understanding of the process.

I would be coming directly from a backpacking weekend and wanted a nearby place to pitch my tent and camp, yet away from commercial zones, restaurants, shops, and the like. I wanted to remain as concentrated and meditational as possible. After much research I found the Sivananda Yoga Farm Ashram. It had everything I needed to reside comfortably: food, showers, open space for tenting. Additionally, it offered daily yoga classes, meditation periods, and lectures. And it was only a ten-minute drive from the ashram to Samadhi, mostly along a winding dirt road through forests and farms. I arrived in the late afternoon, was given the usual orientation, and set off to float. The following is a record of my experiences.

Day One – One Hour

Upon entering the tank for the very first time, I felt I had finally found my home. The water was silky smooth, warm, and comfortable. The immediate sensation was one of returning to a place I had been before and had dearly missed.

Having read Lilly's books, it was obvious to spend the first few moments just relaxing. It did not take long for me to realize, as so many other first-time floaters had mentioned, there was tension in my neck. Allowing the head to tilt a bit farther backward relieved the tension. Arms floated gently along the side. This felt good, so experimenting with other positions wasn't needed. It felt as though the short list of basics was taken care of. There was nothing left to do now but focus completely on relaxing the body deeper and deeper.

The tank seemed to gradually become more silent. And in the deepening silence, eventually it became apparent something was wrong. There was an electrical-sounding buzzing noise. It was hard to tell where exactly it was coming from. Could the tank be making some kind of electrical noise? It took a little while to figure out this was the sound of my own jaw muscles. The tension of holding the jaw closed was causing the muscles to hum. Allowing the jaw to relax and drop a bit quieted the buzzing sound. This was a huge relief. Surely floating in a tank with an electrical noise would not do. Then I realized a bit of ping-ponging was going on. A finger would touch the side of the tank, then a minute later, a toe on the other side. Pushing away gently would only work for so long. A minute or so would pass, then an elbow would touch the other side. After a bit it was obvious this back and forth would not stop unless there was concerted action on my part. I reached out with both hands and feet to the tank sides to center my body and stabilize. Once the inertia of movement completely dissipated, very slowly I allowed the arms and legs to return to their normal relaxed positions. At last I felt all settled in.

I began to think about how exactly I would document this experience. Would I be writing for myself? Would I send my notes to others? How many details would I include? Would I include everything I had experienced in these first few minutes? Then I realized I was overly obsessing and tried to let go of it. I tried to absorb the blackness, the stillness, the quietude. Relaxing even more, my mind began to soften. Suddenly and out of nowhere, the sound of some ethereal instrument. A short musical scale zipped by. It sounded perhaps something like an electric sitar, as though it was inside the tank with me. It was loud, clearly audible, and shocking. Again, I returned to consciously relaxing.

Occasionally there would be other sounds: a single dog bark, a spoken word, or a shout, like "Hey!" I tried to calm my mind and not obsess about all these random, odd little sounds. Suddenly there was a knock at the tank side. This was reality. The hour was up! How amazing and unbelievable! This was an hour-long float? It felt as though it had only been a few minutes. But an even more amazing and peculiar thing was revealed with the knocking. I realized I had been listening to an immense internal chatter. It sounded like an overwhelmingly noisy and busy restaurant, or an auditorium before the curtain was raised. It was the sound of a thousand shouted conversations. However, it did not feel audible like the other sounds from earlier. These voices took the form of thoughts. I had been enveloped in a chorus of boisterous thought on a very deep level, where thought feels electric and is not articulated with the sound of one's voice. I was not conscious of it until the knocking brought me back.

It was already dark outside by the time I arrived at the ashram. The office was locked with lights out, but eventually someone came to open up. I was moving with deep and profound calm in mind and body. As I filled the check-in paperwork, a housefly landed on my knuckle and walked around in circles. I saw it land there, but just continued writing. The Indian lady at the desk was watching, and although she did not respond, I imagined she might think it unusual behavior for a Westerner. I was more tuned in and chilled out than I remember ever being before. I did not mind the little fly investigating. It made three or four circles around my knuckle and flew away. Then I poked my way through the ashram in the dark to find a spot to set up the tent.

Day Two – Two Hours, Fifty Minutes

The morning bell rang at five-thirty for meditation. The ashram has the same rhythm every morning. Formal sitting meditation is at six o'clock with all the other guests, the staff, and the swami in the meditation hall. Then the daily chants are sung, and a spiritual talk is given. The talk lasts almost until nine o'clock. There is a ten-minute break, then a two-hour yoga class. Immediately after is a vegetarian lunch buffet. After lunch, a work assignment is given, and everyone does some job in service of the ashram for an hour.

By one o'clock the daily schedule is finished, and guests either move on to seminars, or have time off to just relax. This is when I would head up the dusty bumpy dirt road through the forest, then a couple miles of pavement passing small farms, and more dirt road to finally arrive at Samadhi. While it may be difficult climbing out of the tent into the cold at five-thirty, after the meditation, lecture, two hours of yoga, beautiful lunch, a little light work, and a scenic drive through the countryside, I felt just wonderful, invigorated, and ready for my second float.

Entering the water, I focused on being perfectly centered and still in the tank. This time, there was no ping-ponging, and no touching sides. I was able to get to a very relaxed state right away. The sound of jaw tension was relieved by allowing the jaw to relax and drop a bit, with the mouth hanging open slightly. It felt good to have the experience from yesterday and be able to just go down the list and settle in within minutes of entering the tank.

With the initial physical business of floating taken care of, it was time to focus on the endeavor that brought me here. Could the levels of thought be clearly evaluated, and what could be found out about the lowest, deepest levels, the source of thought? But soon I was thinking about air. Was it possible that the air was not turned on? Surely they thought of that. But what if they had not? This became a recurring theme for the duration of this float. I would try to forget it and relax, only to wake up startled by the thought that I might suffocate. Occasionally a random scene would present itself. Although the conscious thought process was not aware of it, the subconscious was very much wrapped up in a story line. For instance, I found myself, on a bright sunny day, bent over a cleat on a dock, tying up a small rowboat. I wrapped the rope around the cleat and gave it a final hard yank to set the knot. With that yank, my arm physically jarred to the side, and the water in the tank audibly slapped about. The physical movement woke me to the fact that I had been involved in a fantastic scene, very much not inside the tank. It was more real than any dream I had experienced while sleeping. Then I would be back to wondering about the oxygen. And seemingly minutes later, I would be somewhere else, with another scene outside the tank. I found myself walking down a steep rocky trail. All that was in my vision were the big boulders on the trail, and hiking boots carefully navigating each step downward. Just as a foot was placed in the space between two rocks, my leg physically jarred, the water swashed around, and I realized, I am not on a trail, I am in the tank! At other times, my mind was off somewhere else. Perhaps it was deeply resting. Or perhaps it was busy with something beyond my awareness. At one point, I awoke and thought: "Well, I am still alive, so I probably will not die in here." Overall, I believe I made this full cycle five or more times during this three-hour float. About every thirty minutes I would re-awaken to the fact that I was in a tank, and then, soon enough, I would be gone again, completely oblivious to the existence of the tank. There were many brief glimpses of various situations. These were not long, drawn-out experiences but quick snapshots. I thought of these as pictures of outer reality: outside the tank. Or were they glimpses of inner reality? They certainly felt as real as any outside life activity. The muscles were even involved.

I made it back to the ashram just in time for the afternoon yoga class. The afternoon schedule is sort of a reverse mix of the morning schedule. It starts at four o'clock with two hours of yoga. Immediately afterward a buffet dinner is ready. Then one has about a half-hour break before the seven o'clock meditation, chanting, and spiritual talk. The talk ends by nine o'clock and everyone heads to their sleeping quarters for lights-out time. I had asked to do kitchen cleanup after dinner as my work service, so I could have four hours available mid-day to float. Immediately after dinner, I would go into the kitchen and help wash the enormous pots and pans. Once the kitchen was clean, I would have a brief break, then head off to join everyone for sitting meditation and the rest of the evening program.

Day Three – Three Hours

I awoke with the morning bell at five thirty, attended meditation, chanting, lecture, yoga class, lunch, and drove to Samadhi. Prior to entering the tank today, as with yesterday, I tried to program in an attempt to experience the source of thought. It had not worked out too well yesterday, so today a new approach. Instead of trying to calm my thinking to the point of hearing the early thoughts, maybe I could "sneak up on the deity" by attempting to fully experience the obvious and overt levels first. Begin with vocal out-loud thought, then vocal but non-voiced thought: the thought one hears inside before speaking. Below that, non-vocal thought, the thought with no voice attached, and only then reaching the area in question. Perhaps there are several quieter modes of thinking that could be experienced. And below that, the ultimate goal, the neurochemical impulse that arises out of an experience.

The first hour was spent in the same cyclical realm as yesterday. After passing into quasi-sleep, an image or action of some sort would jar a muscle into response and the waters swashed around for a bit. Then a return to calm waters. Back to relaxing further, mentally leaving the tank again for another outside vision, and repeat. I came to think of this as ping-ponging back and forth across the line of wakefulness. At one point, I realized I had emitted a snore! That frightened me. Heart pounding. A momentary flash of panic. Could I fall asleep in here? Apparently yes! And drown? Probably not, according to the books. But sleep was certainly not my aim. I resolved not to get so wrapped up in thought that I forget where I am. This led to a new mental position in the tank. One of really experiencing what was there: the air, the line of water around the body, the sensation of laying on "something." Most importantly, just being there, and not drifting off into random visions. At least not too much. There were a handful of side travels, but otherwise, focus remained on the present experience. And henceforth, not a single kick or jerk.

I passed my time focusing on breath. As is said in yoga, through the breath comes union. And so, I laid there and breathed.

I was not distracted by random thought. No more sleeping, no more kicking. I experimented with going back to past experiences to see how completely memories might be re-lived inside the tank. I found very vivid and complete records of past events. I went back to a swim I had in Tahiti with many fish and enormous boulders that had been carved into the shape of Polynesian Gods and thrown overboard to rest there. Everything was incredibly vivid. I recalled so much about the boat, the crew, the guests, the little white sand wavelets at the bottom, how people were goofing around in the water. Much more detail came than I had ever remembered about this event. I had the same experience with other memories, and an amusing photographic image of my plate of food from lunch yesterday. Something was achieved here, but what, exactly, I was not sure. Perhaps it was just becoming more present, more focused, less distracted. However, the stated goal, the pursuit of deepest thought, seemed to evade me.

I thought by shutting down my mind, or at least quieting overt thinking, I would be able to exist in the realm of the subconscious. I had expected to be able to enter deep meditation and experience at the level of thoughts becoming, but this was not happening. Instead I would lose control, cross into a hypnagogic state, and my mind would be left to play on its own. The fact that there really are no "experiences" in the tank may have been part of the problem. There is just nothing in there. No light or sound, nothing to feel or smell. That, combined with a meditation practice, and the psyche just dissolves in no time.

Once again, I was back at the ashram just in time for the afternoon yoga class. Doing yoga immediately after a three-hour float is ethereal. At times my field of vision was filled with intricate black and white patterns, to the point I could barely keep my balance. Occasionally it felt as though the yoga I was experiencing was actually one of those mental flashes inside the tank. Sometimes it was hard to tell whether at that instant I was floating and having a mental flash, or actually doing yoga. Practices around the yoga farm were now taking on quite mystical shadings. The waving of the candle before the deities. The blessing of the food before mealtime. Reading "Om Blessed Self" at the top of notices posted

192

in the bathroom. I was being drawn in by it all. I started to join in and sing with everyone else during the daily chants.

Day Four – Three Hours, Ten Minutes

Again, before floating, I recognized and affirmed the goal of calming the layers of thought so as to reach the source of thought in the nervous system. Yet soon after entering the tank, I commenced the usual ping-ponging over the threshold of sleep. At one point of wakefulness, I managed to get a hold of the situation. This ping-ponging must be a very typical beginner level experience. I must focus on the goal!

One of the lectures at the ashram was about all the ways the mind tries to keep us from meditating. It made me think of the techniques I had learned over the years. Normally, when I sit at home, I do not use them in any formal way. Today, I decided to systematically apply them. First, give yourself permission to meditate. Explicitly tell yourself it is OK to be here for twenty minutes, or however long you are going to meditate. Tell yourself that you are now going to meditate, and your goal is to experience a very calm mind and remain in the present moment. Tell yourself, it is OK to let go. Then remind yourself that the mind works in circles, that the same subject comes up over and over. Tell your mind that any subjects or interesting ideas that come up during meditation will not be lost. They will surface again after the meditation session. Allow them to pass during the session. There is no urgency to continue to dwell on any ideas. Nothing will be forgotten.

Another tool for meditation I have found useful is identifying what time period one is thinking about. When you realize your thinking process has been dwelling on one particular subject, simply identify if you are thinking about the past, or the future. Then remind yourself you are here to remain in the present moment. Let go of that other train of thought and make a commitment to only think of the present instant. Acknowledge where you are. Sequentially visualize your location, starting from a macro level all the way down to your meditation cushion.

Think of the planet Earth, then your continent, your region, the neighborhood, the house, the room, the mat, and the cushion you are sitting on. Finally, listen intently. Use your ears to really hear. We have all experienced a moment when a strange sound happens. The mind shuts down immediately, the breath stops, we freeze and just stare, hoping to hear it again and find out what and where it is. This is a close approximation of deep meditation. So, use it. Use your ears to really perceive the moment and shut your thought stream down. Now you are centered, your mind is set, you have your goal, you have a handy tool, and you know it is OK to do this.

In addition, I used the relaxing technique taught at the ashram during yoga class. Relax the toes, the feet, the ankles. Relax the legs, and so forth all the way up to the crown of the head. With this preparation, I began methodically observing and dismissing modes of thought, and fairly quickly the mind reached an extreme calm. This calm lasted as a prolonged, alert, yet relaxed mental state. This was as close to existing with no thought as I had ever experienced. And it lasted for a very long time, perhaps over two hours.

Still there were occasional flashes of random scenes. Mostly now they were undefined. It was hard to place exactly what they were. Some were random shapes, or just so quick the mind could not decipher. One flash though was fantastic and unforgettable. I was standing in a forest, and a deer ran directly toward me. It had dark brown rough shaggy fur, with light tan circles on its forehead and large dots on its back. It was clearly not an animal of this world. It dashed around a bush and almost knocked me over as it passed. Its one eye, centered in a circle of lighter fur, came right up to mine, and for the briefest moment we were eye to eye. It passed me and disappeared in a flash.

My memories of the diving afternoon returned in greater detail. The light streamed through the water down to the sandy bottom. I saw the ripples in the sand like those of a wind-blown sand dune, and the little bits of shells and plants drifting along. I could see the light playing on the face of the white stone God's head. It felt like I was swimming right there. This memory came in detail that was so amazing, I attempted to re-live another event I had been telling a friend about recently.

When I was seven years old, our family took a walk to the corner of Haight and Ashbury. It was the summer of 1968. I would have never remembered all this, with this much detail, with detail finer than I have space to write here, without being in the tank and in this state of mind. Another thing that sparked this particular memory was that the ashram had shown a movie about the founder. He was surrounded by hippie-yogis in the 1960s and flew around the continent in a small plane painted by Peter Max. My family was about as suburban square as one could possibly imagine at that time, with our crew cuts and windbreakers. Mom had just a hint of a beehive hairdo. We were driving a big brown station wagon on a family vacation from Orange County to Yosemite, Lake Tahoe, and San Francisco. Along the way, my parents gave in to the constant pressure from my older brothers, who were in their mid-teens, and took us to see the hippies in Haight-Ashbury.

We found a parking space on a side-street two blocks away from the famed corner. We walked past the coolsters, who were pretty much gawking at us as much as we were at them, and walked straight to the signpost. There were two hippie girls in their teens, dressed cool with their vests, beads, and feathers, sitting on the sidewalk right under our feet. They were leaning against the building with legs straight out on the sidewalk. I noticed them right at the instant they saw us coming. They stubbed out a joint just as we walked up to the signpost. We stopped, looked at it, and looked around. I smiled a little at the girls. My family was awkwardly not saying much and just standing there in a circle. Then one of the girls sort of whispered out loud at me, trying for no-one else to hear: "Hey, little boy." I did not really hear her at first. Then I realized and looked straight at her. She smiled big and half whispered, and half mouthed, with a crazy whimsical expression: "Hey—little boy! Isn't it a beautiful day?" I did not know what to think of that. My mother must have heard something. She demanded I tell her what the girl said. I looked at them, looked at my mom, and said I did not know. My parents then marched us all back to the station wagon.

Once in a while, I reflect on that question: "Isn't it a beautiful day?" It has only popped out of my memory once every couple of decades since. And usually I only remember the two girls, and the question, not the whole scene as I relived it in the tank. But that question! It is stated as a negative! "Is it not a beautiful day?" And the rhythm of the way she said it: "Isn't it – a beauty – full day?" Is it not full of beauty, this day? I am just thrilled the memory of this day, and those two girls, has been brought back to me in such incredible detail.

Back at the ashram, I sensed this afternoon that I have always been here, that I would rather be nowhere else, that there is no point in any other lifestyle. Of course, I knew I have not always been here, and that there is very real life waiting for me at home, and my responsibilities in my regular life are important. What was being expressed inside of me was simply a very free, peaceful, appreciative mode of being. It is so fulfilling it feels as if I could give up all else. Right here, right now. In the evening, the ashram began a program focused on recovery. The attendees had dealt with, or were dealing with, extremely disheartening situations and addictions. Some of the stories and discussions are very sad. This all brings me back to earth very quickly. These talks really deflate my state of highness. By morning, I feel fairly normal, and somewhat detached from the whole experience. It feels as though I am only here to accomplish the goal, and not get caught up in the mysticism and emotion of the place.

Day Five – Three Hours

Today I really focus right at the start on the layers of thought and trying to quiet each. I use my meditation techniques, and the ones being taught at the ashram. I use the yogic progressive relaxation technique progressing from toes to head. While acknowledging my location, I ponder the black box. The utter blackness inside. Then think of the world outside. The room just outside the tank door. Outside that room, another room. Beyond that room, the yard. Past the yard, another yard, and another building. The local neighborhood, and the local region. Then there is the greater geographical region, the continent, the oceans.

The globe itself is outside the door. And why stop there? Outside the tank door is not only this planet, but the others in our solar system, and beyond that, our galaxy, and the countless galaxies beyond. All this is outside the tank door. The endless matter of all the universe is outside the tank door. Ultimately, this entity floating inside the tank is actually floating inside a tank located in a place which is at the very center of the entire known universe.

Once I finished all that, and amused, I commenced. The vocal layers are gone immediately. Lower layers are very still right away. But the flashes continue. I approach sleep, but not as much as prior days. Today the flashes are not so much things I am doing as just random images. Mostly not recognizable, but images nonetheless, and I still move slightly in reaction, but not as much of a jerking motion as before. After about an hour of ping-ponging between flashes and thinking about not thinking, I was able to decide to not flash so much, and get into the layers of thought more, and calm those down even further. I reached very quiet modes of thinking very quickly. At one point, it occurred to me that the brain just sparks these random flashes at will, and periodically. The longer I lay there, the more they subsided, until they only happened once every five minutes or so. And so, I was able to really reach some profoundly quiet states of mind.

I saw a flash of white, with black symbols on it. I saw wavy lines which turned into circles. I saw a lot of geometric objects I could not recognize. They looked like pieces of furniture, but not shapes we would be familiar with. Toward the last hour, I was resting in very quiet mind. At one point, the sensation of water and air became more like a sensation of some undefined liquid below and some undefined liquid above, as if I was sandwiched between two layers of thick liquid. My mind was almost completely blank.

Though hard to imagine, the darkness of the tank seemed to become even darker. My breathing slowed to just very occasional lifting of the chest. When the breathing reaches this very relaxed slow-motion mode, the water in the tank does not move. Everything descends into absolute stillness. The quiet then seems to get magnitudes quieter. My thinking had slowed even more than my breath.

All seemed otherworldly. It felt as though, without sitting up, or using the tank door, I could reach my arm straight up, open some imaginary cosmic door, and step straight ahead and out into the light. I tried doing that in my imagination but, sadly, did not go anywhere. In this absolute deepest of deep non-thought, I perceived a sort of etheric record player. A spark of electricity was flowing from the needle on the raised arm to the vinyl. More just a flow of electric blue plasma through the air than a spark. And the record was slowly turning at around five RPM. This plasma I felt as well as saw. My psyche was etching its way along the record with a flow of blue arcing plasma. It felt and looked very much like an image of the Akashic Record, with my very soul being slowly burnt into it. It was not like watching some sort of slide show or light show: the flashes were momentary and far between, brief glimpses between long spans of nothingness. As an overlay to the mind quieting techniques I was practicing, these flashes were startling.

My existence at the ashram was now almost vanishing. Yoga is otherworldly. I eat dinner quietly off by myself somewhere. My mind is beyond calm. I sit at the back of the hall for meditation, and duck out as the lecture starts. Walking through the grounds, it is night, and the stars are glistening. Deer slowly walk nearby. I ponder the six-hour float that is coming tomorrow. Arrangements had been made, in the tradition of the inventor. I ponder the psychogenic catalyst, a tiny jar containing liquid LSD as clear and transparent as spring water. It is here now, am I ready?

Day Six – Session One – Three Hours

Could I die here?

Focus on breath,
Breath, the way to union.

Union of what with what?
This consciousness with that of all humanity?
All the space in the universe with the space in this tank?

Breathing slower, relaxing jaw, so to release the sound of muscles
straining.

Heart beating,
Breathe, relax jaw, relax body, tilt head back, breathe,
Feeling the tank waters settling in,
Breath is the key to union.

Union of what with what?
All of space with this space?
All mind with this mind?

Thinking of that stone head laying in sand,
A strange submerged monolith in the waters of Tahiti,
A white stone head, intricately carved and thrown overboard,
To lie forever on its back, under the waters, staring upward,
Blue-green wavelets dancing about overhead,
Rippled soft white sand below,
Staring upward,
Little fish floating about.

Its creators playing and plopping about in the joyous waters,
and staring down at it from above.

Breathing very slowly now, sound of heart beating,
adjusting jaw to stop muscle noise.

Blue waters, ever so blue,
Stone God head laying in sand,
staring upward.

What's that sound?
A humming, buzzing sound, zooming downward, then up!
Cutting through some cosmic substance, shimmering through
layers,
Some kind of cosmic synthesizer,
Now a barrel roll.

Remember to breathe!
Have I been breathing at all?
Heart thumping, synthesizer zooming, God head laying in sand,
Sunlight playing on the sandy bottom,
And streaming through the waters all around,
Surface of water above gently rippling everywhere,
Cosmic synthesizer, humming, gliding along,
Cutting through layers like giant onion, zip-zip-zip-zip-zip
A lazy dripping sound cutting through,
Cutting through choppy ripples.

Breathe...breathe.
Relax jaw,
Relax body,
Adjust head,
Ever slower breath, imperceptible breath,
If anywhere, intergalactic communication must be possible here.

Little fish floating along, silvery slivers,
Peering into silvery scales, God head,
What colors in those scales!
Pink, blue, red!
Is that the blue of ever so blue tropical waters?
The pink of pinkest coral?
The red of sunset?
So many colors in that fish scale!
Now silver, now scales, now flashes of every tropical color.

And what is this?
A pencil point?
A melting ice cone?
A pointing upward, into blue, blue tropical water sky,
Icy melting cap, in white, but reflecting intense sky blue,
melting, melting, and pointing upward to endless blue sky.
And what's this now?
Himalayan peaks?
Ever so high, ever so high, white rugged peaks tall to the sky,

The highest peaks in this world.

Higher yet, here am I, floating high above,
The Himalayan blue sky, white snow covered peaks,
Pencil point ice cones melting,
Colors of blue and red and pink, silver fish scales,
God head laying, staring upward, its creators swimming about,
Making faces down at him.

Have I been breathing at all?
Take a nice slow breath, could I die here?
Just forget to breathe?
And pass on, into the blue, into the blackness,
a gentle passing.

Breathe,
Breathe,
Relax…relax.

And the red, is that the red of Himalayan sunset?
Red, pink, orange, huge white peaks shaded in sunset colors.

And my legs and arms, thick and stubby, bejeweled,
Laced with finest cloth, I'm the lion of the gates,
Pawing about, floating above the tallest mountains in the world, at
sunset, Lion pawing at air.

And this?
This goddess?
Lying here alongside?
Finest garments, finest jewels, deepest burnt orange skin, Lakshmi?
Durga?
Merging arms and legs,
Tiger merging, with Deity.
Breathe!
Am I breathing at all?
Remember to breathe, and relax into it,

Back down under sea, blue shimmering joyous waters,
Blue Himalayan sky, cosmic synthesizer,
Silvery endless layers of fish scale.

Breath in, hold, breath out, union!
Stone head staring to surface, Himalayan skies,
How high the peaks!
How gentle the waters!
Synthesizer gliding and peeling along!

And the green garden of Sivananda, at the sunset, warm summer
sunset,
Lush lumps of growing substance, tall green corn stalks,
Trees and bushes all about, and lush dark green food,
Food, alive and growing.

And the garden child, tending the soil, pointy straw hat,
Brown skin, shaved head, tan clothes,
Earth child, merging with garden, peace all around,
Raking at nothingness.

Now synthesizer, now Polynesian God, now melting icy cones,
Take it all in with a slow gentle breath.

Surrounded by unimaginable color, burnt orange, intense red and
blue,
Emerald garden green, pink, tropical water blue,
All in a silver fish scale.

And the Goddess wide open above, blistering wide open sexuality,
The Gods merging, in sky, and sea.

Has none died here?
Just forgotten to breathe?
It could have gone on and on, and there must be so much more,
Endless images.

Now to remember as much as possible,
To bring tales back from the blackness,
Back from the tank, to the outer world.

I reflect on the teachings of Buddha, stopping short of final
liberation,
So as to save others.

And having done that, returning, going further,
Returning to pinnacle of existence, vanishing off into pure
enlightenment.

So I return to breath, and try to collect myself,
Having ridden this roller-coaster, what else?
What beyond these sensuous images?

Return to my stated goal — the task of letting go of thought.
Return to the blackness, and let go thinking, layer after layer.
Relax further, breathe ever more slowly, barely taking in air.

Listening intently, is that a pulse of thought?
Relax it, and listen, turning off mind.

I have not had the flashes of images today, no jerks to action,
All that seems to have been released now,
Like so many popcorn kernels, all the little stresses,
Gone, all popped off,
Nothing left of stress, nothing left of ego, just lying here in the
blackness,
Lying on these black waters,
Nothing left.

How slow and slight can breath be?
Will I pass on?
Long spans of lungs resting empty,
Yet remember to breathe on occasion,

And relax.
Mind lying low, it seems easy to just expire now, nothing left.

Then, an ascending, through black curving tunnel, upward,
Birth canal in reverse, up the tube, returning to the womb,
Warm black damp cavern.

Then, an open space, a landing,
Somehow perceived through this absolute pitch black,
There are others here,
They too having relaxed all tension, left off ego, expired,
They are here, communing in the silence, existing together,
Sitting in a large circle, as if attending a cosmic meeting of souls,
Some are very old, thousands, millions of years,
Others are very new, yet practicing, and somehow achieving this
    state,
Meditating, and sharing the most minimal act, of mere presence.

Now I know where I am, this is it, this is where we go,
When we find deepest meditation, at the very edge of death,
The threshold, easy to cross.

And then, I realize a most profound entity,
At the center of this circle of beings, there is The One!
A black orb, God's soul, hanging there above us all,
The eternal soul, Brahman himself!
Without beginning, without end.
The ancient souls, and I, sit in a circle below Him,
The meeting has commenced.

I feel the vacuum of His existence, and as empty as I am at this
moment,

Not empty enough, it's just too much, now more than I can take,
How can I be here in the presence of God!
In the presence of the court of highest souls!
Surely, I have more work to do, to deserve.

As immediately as these thoughts arise, the tunnel collapses,
An eviction, an evaporation, all gone,
Almost as though thought itself erased the vision.

I now play in and out of this state of relaxation,
Thinking about the experience, then calming, remembering to
breathe,
Imperceptible slow breaths, ascending to union.

I need more time in here, to experience this, to explore these
    ancient souls,
However, my body has other needs. I must take a short break.
Coming to rise from the waters, dripping sound all around,
Reaching for the door, just a crack to let enter white light,
To throb at my eyes.

Day Six - Session Two - Two Hours

Soon I am diving back in, two more hours in the tank.

Before turning back to non-thought, to the task at hand,
I recite my gratitude...

Thank you, Samadhi, thank you, Sivananda, thank you, Lilly,
Thank you, garden child!

To all my teachers: Shihan, Sensei, Cho Bo Zen Ji, Tassajara, John
Childers,
Thank you!

To my friends: Thank you, guides along this path.
Thank you: Kesey, Watts, Kerouac, Ishaya!

To those that prepared me for this journey: my brothers, the dead,
the springfield, the fish, thank you!

To my parents: ma ma ma ma ma ma - pa pa pa pa pa, thank you!

Krishna, Shiva, Brahman, Vishnu, Buddha, thank you!

Thank you, Yoga Farm.

Thank you, all,
Om shanti, shanti, shanti,
Om peace, peace, peace.

That evening, landing ever so softly, surrounded by all that is
the ashram. In the kitchen, dutifully carrying out my task of
washing the giant communal pots and pans. Keeping low and
just washing, trying not to attract any attention to my state of
highness, controlling and subduing wave after wave of ecstasy
inside. And feeling comfortable, assured that acting this way is
in no way whatsoever different than how I, and everyone else,
acts normally all the time, in the protected ashram environment.
Washing the pot, washing the pan. Drying, stacking. In a kitchen
which experiences nothing but incredible sattvic Hindu vegetarian
substance. With the orange and purple sunset peeking through the
valley, the trees, the screen door. On the kitchen CD player, some
sacred band softly playing devotional music. And then later, deep
blue dusk with stars gleaming, the clanging bell calling everyone to
the hall to meditate and chant. Following along the path through
the lawn...still tripping just a little...incredibly fine and precious,
immaculate, ecstatic.

As I sat in the meditation hall, I spotted that black egg-
shaped rock on the altar. My jaw almost dropped. I recognized
it immediately and got a shock of adrenalin. That was the exact
shape of what I had experienced in the blackness! It is the form of
the soul of God! I had seen it before on altars, at yoga studios, in
images. Just an odd artifact that I didn't understand. Now I could
not wait to ask someone, anyone—but someone with authority,
like senior staff, or a swami—what they think that rock represents.
Surely it cannot be!

The evening reading is about what transpires when one

206

achieves deepest levels of meditation, how the breath slows until it becomes imperceptible, how the mind becomes free of its movement, how one travels upward leaving body and world behind, and comes into the presence of Brahman, joining the unbounded cosmos. This described exactly what I had experienced in the tank that day. I was astounded, and simply could not believe how the reading this evening could so precisely describe what I had just experienced! And equally as unbelievable, how could this reading be timed to the very day it happened for me! It was all I could do to just stay seated there, silently, and smile. Inside, I wanted to jump up and yell out, like a crazed Zen monk upon his realization. I wanted to tell everyone it is true—and that black rock is exactly what Brahman looks like! When the evening ended, I enquired, and was told the black rock is the Siva Lingam, the abstract form of Shiva. I held back countering that this is the very real, indisputable, form of Shiva's soul!

An Intermission

The next day I stopped by Samadhi to chat and to say my good-byes, and to give them my heartfelt thanks for the amazing journey. I told Lee that I would be back very soon. I was absolutely possessed with the vision of Shiva Lingam. I had to attempt to revisit the universal mind state I had reached on day six, only this time without the sacrament. Lee told me these types of experiences are usually a one-time deal, that it is hard to recreate one's visions. I was not convinced. If this thing is so real that it sits on almost every Hindu temple altar in the world, then surely it can be revisited. It is not the recreation of a vision, it is returning to a place, and the souls, that exist in this cosmos.

I also needed confirmation that what I had experienced was indeed the Siva Lingam. I had to get back to the ashram and enquire of those who know. What exactly was it that I experienced? Do people really leave their body and travel up a black tunnel, and arrive at a group of souls, and experience God in the form of that black rock? And if the experience is accurate, does it matter how a person got there? Yogis in India lay on beds of nails and perform all manner of austerities. Is it not orthodox to lay on a bed of saltwater? The seers of ancient times used intense doses of tobacco. Is a substance that assists one directly to God to be shunned?

As I made my way five hundred miles homeward, I felt as though I was a different person. I was firmly grounded, and at peace. I had seen things few walking this earth could imagine. And upon arriving home, I immediately planned a second trip back to Grass Valley.

Two months later, I departed again for a new seven-day series of floats. I planned to log over thirty hours of tank time. Last time, I floated eighteen hours in six days, including five hours on day six. Lee at Samadhi thought eighteen hours in six days, for someone with no prior floating experience, might have been record-breaking. In the meantime, the result of my experience with the ashram and floatation was clear and immediate. My morning meditation was far advanced from where it had been. I now knew where one goes when the mind and nervous system is emptied, and I felt sure of the technique for gaining that state. My aim for this next trip was to reinforce and expand this experience. I wanted to revisit Lilly's Level +3 State, arrive there sooner than on day six, and remain in that state for a longer time. And I felt certain this state could be experienced without the use of a chemical trigger.

The eight-hour drive passed very quickly. There was no confusion on the back roads. A simple left, right, left, and a left onto the dirt road. I arrived at the yoga farm around 10:30 PM. After check-in, I wandered around for a while in the dark looking for a tent site. It was a beautiful evening.

Day Seven - Two Hours, Fifty Minutes

As usual, I partook in morning meditation, chanting, lecture, yoga, breakfast, and then headed off to float. It seemed difficult to stay focused. Thought calmed to non-vocal levels after about an hour. I was able to leave off memories somewhat, and had many flashing images which occurred so quickly before my mind that I could not tell what they were. Some were abstract rectangular objects with jagged lines of black, red and white. Some were recognizable things or situations. I was too tired to concentrate on my program of achieving deepest meditation and realization of universal mind. Too tired to concentrate even on what thought levels I was experiencing or on the practice of listening to thought. It must have been the long drive and late arrival, as well as all the scrambling over the previous few weeks to get the house ready for my fiftieth birthday party. So, I just let it be and relaxed and soaked in the Epsom salts. I thought of it as an "ordinary float," what someone with no meditation practice might experience. I snored a few times. I just let the mind do its thing. Afterward, I felt good and relaxed, and calm.

Day Eight - Three Hours

On arrival at Samadhi Tank Company, I talked with Lee about the possibility of dying in the tank: just forgetting to breathe. As it is said, a yogi can do this when they have completed the things they were born to do and are ready to leave this world. I felt very close to being able to do this intentionally on day six of my first series of floats. I felt as though I could just stop the breathing process and expire. The question was, could this happen unintentionally? Lee related what John Lilly had said: "While you are in the tank, the instructions for what you need to live are in the glove box. When you need that program, it is there. In the tank, nobody is going anywhere. Nobody is getting out, and nobody is getting in. This formulation was arrived at after many years of floating experience." I trusted this information and could enter the tank satisfied that I would not be departing this life by accidentally going too far in meditation.

Now in the tank, at first there were lots of flashing images. I set the program "no projections" and they stopped immediately. However, my mind just did not want to stop. There was no sleeping, but constant thinking. There were a few very brief passes near no-thought. Counting breaths during the last thirty minutes got me much closer to meditation. But it seemed to be a struggle. I knew what I needed to do. I had to really focus on keeping a calm mind between now and tomorrow's float. Walk slowly and avoid unnecessary conversation. Remain meditative and speak only when absolutely necessary to perform my duties.

At the ashram they began a week-long Yoga Sutras,

Meditation, and Silence retreat. Considering my desire to remain calm, this could not have come at a better time. Once again, as had happened many times before, events at the ashram seemed to provide what I needed at the moment. Many attendees took a vow of silence. I was hopeful that a lot of the usual conversation would go away. The evening lecture was about the eight limbs of yoga, and "focus" having the meaning "restriction." Like a goat leashed to a pole, it can only wander so much. One uses mantra to achieve this. Bring the mind back with OM. This is what I needed to hear, and I began the practice. Everywhere I went and everything I did was accompanied by my repeating Om Om Om inside my head.

Day Nine - Three Hours

At morning satsang, the reading described how during deepest meditation the breath is barely moving. Just the diaphragm moves occasionally. This is exactly what I had experienced before on day six and was the reason for my concern about passing away in that state. It was amazing and reassuring to hear this was written about by Swami Sivananda so very long ago. Also, a technique was given: "Focus mind on the goal. Focus on Brahman, universal mind. Think of nothing else." This technique had not occurred to me. The ashram was very peaceful that morning. There were no loud conversations or banging around. People were moving slowly. If ever, this was the week to be here.

At Samadhi, I talked with Lee for quite a while. I told her many stories of my earlier life. We may have talked for an hour, with me doing most of the talking. Afterward, I knew this was a mistake. None of it was forced, and I love talking with my hosts. However, the goat got loose. I let go of my focus on calm and quiet. And in the tank, I spent the entire float rehashing my life. It was very difficult to shut off my mind. OM did not work. The float was irritating and seemed a waste of time. On exiting I went to Lee and requested silence for a few days as I came and went. She understood and was wholeheartedly supportive of this request.

At the ashram I saw the priest who lives there walking along a pathway. I hurriedly caught up to him to ask about my day six vision. I told him I was meditating laying on my back in the yogic shvasana position for many hours. My mind and breathing had almost stopped. I did not fall asleep but had a vision of being drawn up a black tunnel. I felt the presence of other beings, and in the center, I thought I saw the Shiva Lingum hanging above us all. I asked, "Did I really see Shiva?" He looked quickly into my eyes, and nodded in affirmation: "Yes, that is Shiva." He turned away and briskly continued down the path.

Day Ten - Three Hours

In the tank, my heart was pumping hard, despite calm breath. I focused intently on calm mind and seemed to be able to let go of mental threads instantly. My thinking was not as bothersome as yesterday. Eventually my heart calmed down. I felt ever closer to the goal of universal mind but I was not quite there yet. On exiting the tank, I was extremely detached from the world and thought.

Later, at the ashram, walking along the road through the evening sunlight, with mind almost blank, my sandal kicks up a small white pebble. It spins like a top for a moment, then stops dead instantly. The clockwork nature of this event strikes my mind as an example of the laws of physics: inertia, motion, rotational velocity; the set of natural laws that make up the Tao itself; that everything, the planets, the flesh growing on the goat standing nearby, the grass blowing in the wind, everything is governed by these laws. Everything. And yet there is also chaos, and random interaction. All this matter following the laws that govern in a very orderly fashion, yet everything is colliding randomly. A fascinating reflection on reality, thanks to a little pebble in the road.

Day Eleven – Five Hours, Thirty Minutes

My heart was pounding very loudly. I tried everything to diminish the hammering sound and could not turn off mind with this constant thumping in my ears. Tried the relaxation practice: no help. Tried OM which helped somewhat, but only if I OM to the rhythm of my heart. As soon as I began to leave off body sensations, I would leave off OM and be right back to the thumping again. Tried mantra, visualizations of deities, visualization of the symbol OM. No help. I began to see an orange peel texture somewhere before me. It was colored grey and faded in and out. Sometimes little groups of pimples pushed out of it and then receded. Sometimes other shapes appeared on it for a moment.

At about two hours forty-five minutes I tried to tune into visual patterns and make them happen. Anything to distract myself from the heart pounding. This became interesting enough to keep me in the tank for another two hours. But it was still hard to do even this. Back to relaxation practice. Tried to sleep. Tried just letting the tank take me wherever it wanted. Interesting effects, but still the pounding continued. Finally, I try putting my attention firmly into the heart chakra. And there it is! Peace! At last! Wow. The pounding was surely as physically intense, but mentally it did not seem to bother me at all. It seemed natural and healthy now. What a relief! The orange peel now surrounded me completely. My body expanded to fill the limits of the orange peel space. I relaxed and enjoyed this relief. It seemed just a few minutes later that the knock at the tank came.

On exit, profound calm and detachment. I sat in the car and did not want to go anywhere. Just watching the trees and grass was more than enough. I could have sat there the rest of the evening, just watching.

Day Twelve – Six Hours, Thirty Minutes

I had a wonderful flash of a gold and copper tile mosaic. Each tile felt to be about one-inch square. They reflected a warm dark golden light. This mosaic brought much emotion with it. Soon I was thinking about various deities and the lavish surroundings they exist within. For a while I thought about the interconnectedness of the various major religions. The Muslim culture has fantastic mosaic art, and weaving. The Hindu cosmos has incredibly creative stories and characters. And the Buddhists have their impossible puzzles to spend months pondering. What is the common cosmic vision?

I began thinking about my upcoming birthday and all the

people that would be at the party. Many interesting talents would be represented there. What connections could be made between these people? Who should be introduced to whom? And who else could be invited to fill out the web of connections? What sort of organizations could be formed with all these people? I thought about my career path. I decided to seriously enquire about the yoga teacher certification course at the ashram, and formulated a series of questions. Almost the entire float was spent in this mode of planning and considering aspects of my life. It did not feel like a waste of time. It felt productive. At the end, I took a few minutes to practice meditation. The mind calmed quickly. It felt good.

In the evening at the ashram we were shown a movie about the Fire Yogi of Tanjore. I now think of my floatation experiences as that of being the Epsom Salts Yogi. I go off to my box, lie in the darkness and quiet, and float on the salts to meditate. It is a lot more comfortable than a bed of nails, and certainly more so than a fired oven. Is it truly necessary to endure inhuman extremes of pain to achieve the goal? Is not finding a quiet and comfortable place to meditate natural enough?

Day Thirteen – Four Hours

I had a hard time sleeping last night. My body seemed too sore to get in a good position, knees sore from sitting so long at meditation and satsang every day. Awake most of the night. Maybe I had too much tea at dinner.

In the tank, trying to meditate. Sleeping sort of half-way. A weird state of being awake, barely, and yet snoring. The whole snoring thing was unusual for me. I think it happens in the tank because of the angle of my head, and the position I leave my jaw and tongue in so there is not the sound of muscle tension. But snoring while partially awake is really strange. I seem to make no progress. Try something new. Open eyes, open ears. As if unfamiliar with the tank, try to sense if it is "working." Is it truly silent? Is it truly dark? Pretending I had built it and was testing it for the first time. What was I experiencing? This brought me closer to the meditative state. I relaxed into it. The water became very calm. The flashing images returned. My legs and arms jarred

213

in response to some of them. I saw snowy mountain peaks with intense blue skies. I saw a vivid green treed slope reaching up the base of a huge rocky and snowy mountainside. It was spring, warm and gentle. I did not see but felt the presence of flowers in the trees. It could be Kashmir, soothing and warm. This felt more like astral travel than I had ever experienced. I entered a good solid meditative state for a long time.

Day Fourteen – Four Hours

Glenn at Samadhi told me one of John Lilly's sayings: "Do not get attached to anything, and do not push anything out. Just explore." The practice of letting go of thoughts is working well today. I return countless times to calm mind. I stay calm for long periods. At one point it occurred to me that my mental states had reversed. It felt as if having a thinking process running was the altered state, and a calm un-thinking mind was the normal state: the reverse of my normal experience where a calm mind feels like the altered state. This seemed a revelation. The last hour in the tank was almost entirely a state of pure empty mind, the deepest and longest meditation I have ever experienced. On occasion, I would wake up to my body and environment and think, "How strange, to be floating in this black box." Then I would let that go and be right back to deep meditation. On exit, I did not want to drive. I just wanted to sit somewhere and observe the Dao.

The One That Got Away

Upon arriving home after this series of floats, I was most happy just cooking or puttering around in the garden by myself. My mind and body were very relaxed. I really enjoyed being alone. It was an extraordinary experience. I felt I was in the process of changing my life. Indeed, my life was changing. This afterglow lasted many weeks.

I returned to the ashram for teacher training later that same year. And every year since I have returned to the ashram and to float at Samadhi Tank Company. My life path was being massaged into a new form.

As to exploring the deep unconscious, down to the level of

the genesis of thought, I was not able to achieve that experience inside the tank. If I were an archer, and my aim was a bullseye, one could say the arrow fell afield. However, other experiences, equally as spiritually engaging, were bestowed. As if a fisherman intent on landing a marlin caught a sunfish instead. It is not the exact fish he was after, but one equally if not more beautiful. It may come down to the fact that inside the tank there are no objects to trigger one's senses. All those years ago, when I experienced the formation of thoughts, I was not isolated but in the real world, with the objects of the world around me. I had been meditating a lot over a period of several months and using the listening technique to quiet the thought process. Just observing the psyche's reaction to the various objects around me had led to a profound experience.

A friend had left town for a few days, and I was housesitting. There was a table, a figurine, a vase: just normal stuff. I noticed that as an object came into my field of vision, my body would respond to it physically. It would start as a sort of electrical current, somewhere near the solar plexus. It felt almost like the adrenaline one feels when surprised suddenly. This reaction was extremely subtle, almost imperceptible, triggered at the sight of an object. As the current rose through my body, it would pick up tiny bits of emotion. I came to think of this emotion as the residue of previous experiences. Even though I had never seen some of these objects in the room, as my senses reacted to them, bits of stored emotion from previous experiences with similar objects were triggered. The electrical impulse continued to rise and to collect bits of emotion. Eventually enough bits were collected that the impulse had an emotional overtone. Gradually the force of emotion would cause the impulse to form into an almost-verbal expression. Almost verbal, but not quite yet. The expression was more in the form of a primate's grunt, language at a pre-verbal level. The grunt continued to evolve as the impulse rose until it took on the form of a human word. That word became the first building block of a thought, on the deep subconscious level. And after that, an actual thought would form about the object, on a level where thoughts feel like intuition.

Many years later I learned that Hindu philosophy calls the

residue of previous experience samskara. I now believe what I was experiencing was the initial electro-chemical reaction being colored by samskara. And as the reaction rose through the nervous system, samskara continued to collect until the reaction became a thought. It became obvious that the tone of the stored samskara was the basis of the resulting thought. Deeply stored negative emotions would push the impulse toward negatively flavored thinking, and positive toward positive. I found that the experience of this process was not repeated inside the tank. Perhaps because there are no objects to react to. Without objects to react to, the mind either conjures memories, or creates fantastic visions, fanciful combinations of random bits of memory. Perhaps the spirit of God moving upon the waters is actually sensory input striking the lake of stored impressions in the nervous system. Without sensory input, I could not duplicate the experience of this particular path of thought creation. However, thoughts and images were most certainly created, some of them very meaningful.

Another fish was soon to be caught. In the following years, my continued use of the floatation tank at Samadhi, combined with the deep spiritual practices at the Yoga Farm, led to further insights. On one occasion at the ashram, I did experience the effect of samskara in a slightly different, yet extremely meaningful way. I had been residing at the ashram for a couple of weeks, attending a "Yoga Intensive" retreat, and floating at Samadhi as much as I could in the time off. My mind had reached a level of calm beyond any I had experienced before. I had gone beyond even the calm of the first fourteen-day series. I was in a constant state of meditation. But something was driving me absolutely crazy. I realized that everything I looked at triggered its name. My meditation was far too deep to react with likes and dislikes, or descriptions of any other kind. However, I could not stop the mind from reacting by conjuring the name of each item I saw. I would walk around, and at each thing before me, I would instantly apply a name. All I would hear inside was: "Tree. Leaf. Sun. Pebble. House." It was driving me nuts.

Finally I went to a swami for advice. His answer was to meditate with the mantra: repeat "Om Om Om" in every action, and all the time.

Eventually the impulse to name things shut down. Now, there was nothing inside at all, a completely empty state with no thought whatsoever. This was the void. Instantly a rush of bliss washed through me like none I have ever known. It was pure ecstasy to be able to exist without the mind moving. Simply absorbing everything around without reacting in any mental way. Bliss is the only way to describe this feeling of pure existence. It felt so amazing. It felt almost too good. My body's first spontaneous reaction was to raise from somewhere deep within a feeling of guilt about feeling so blissful. I was not ready for this level of goodness. How incredibly disheartening to think I had worked so hard, finally shut off the mind, entered the realm of true unaltered bliss, and my psyche reacted with a swell of guilt!

I had to find out more about this mechanism. Is this a typical reaction for a novice experiencing the bliss world? Is there a way to prevent this reaction? I immediately sought out the counsel of the swami. The answer was, until you have removed your karma, your past will cause you to feel guilty. And how is that to be fixed? Through selfless service to others. Only by karma-yoga can one clean up the toxic karmic residue. And so, the challenge before me was to find a way to serve others and wash my psyche.

I was not told so specifically at this time, but it was logical to think the next step would be to remove further guilt by giving away all of one's possessions, become free of every trace of materialism, and live the life of a renunciate. Normally, the motivation of the renunciate is incomprehensible. How and why would a person give up this material life and live with only a simple cloth wrapping the body, barefoot, and in constant prayer, residing at an ashram or other spiritual community? This now made perfect sense to me. For one to reside in the deepest levels of meditation, and not experience negative side effects, one needs to become as pure as possible.

If one has the desire to exist in the presence of the God, to sit with Saraswati, Lakshmi, and the other high beings who reside along God's side, then one must learn to release all tension, release all motive, and let the psyche be stripped down to one's very soul.

And to exist in the state of utmost bliss, as is heralded by the songs of the saints, one must learn to release oneself of the bonds of karma. It is said there are other paths besides that of renunciation. It is also considered honorable to be a householder, remaining at home, taking care of one's family, and working for the good of the local community. This is also considered a valid path to realization. This world needs both the householder and the guru to provide the means for every being to explore their destiny.

Float Experience
Wayne Silby

In the early 1980s I was running a mutual fund I had co-founded and we were becoming quite successful. We were able to pay higher interest than the banks as we invested into the higher yielding money market instruments. As a result, our customers got better yields from us than they received from the banks, who were limited by regulation. The banks were quite jealous as people were withdrawing money from the banks and placing it with us. Our company was growing very fast as money rolled in and we were hiring many people and investing in expensive computer systems to track all the money.

The banks started complaining to the government about this situation and began lobbying the regulators to change the laws to allow them to pay higher interest rates than we could pay (which resulted in the money market deposit account still available today at many banks). The banks got the law changed and people started moving their money from us back to their bank. I think there was one hundred million dollars in withdrawals in the first month of the new law. This meant we were going from fast growth to the real risk of imploding! We had about one hundred fifty people hired in the four years we were in business and now everyone's job was at risk. All eyes were on me as to what to do! I felt the pressure. This is when I got the idea that I needed a float tank.

I needed something to help me collect and focus my energies. I was so worried I could hardly sleep. I felt the internal jitters and had a hard time thinking straight. I needed to be more like a Zen warrior than a monkey mind out of control. So, desperate, I ordered a tank from Samadhi thinking it might get me more calm and centered.

The instructions from Samadhi on how to set up the tank were, alone, an exercise in crafted detail. I could feel the caring of those who put them together, as if they were speaking to me in a gentle voice. I had a good feel I was on a fruitful path. The first float was very calming. I could have my worries but they were not controlling me as I just concentrated on the breath. On later floats, I just let my mind go. And then an idea started to bubble up. It was like my mind was a neuro net, a holistic access into my diverse thoughts just below the conscious surface. And then an idea came to me.

It was so counterintuitive, that we could join with the banks instead of trying to compete with them. They really wanted our customer money more than the customers themselves. I realized there was a way we could just give them the money as agents for our customers. Our customers, with our help, could now switch back to the familiar insured FDIC bank program but with us acting as their agents. We found banks willing to pay the account holders the higher rates while also paying us a service fee. Well, within six months, we had almost six hundred million in that program and it saved our company! And amazingly, we made more on the service charges than we had been making on the management fees!

I continued to use my float tank for various far out creative endeavors. Not just for ideas, but testing out those ideas in the expansive space a tank offers. It was a way to take visions and run them forward into the future and to challenge them over time to evaluate their practicality. One idea I had was for a mutual fund that represented the values of my 60s generation. From that was born the first comprehensive social investment fund launched in the USA, Calvert (the name of the street we were on), which became a multi-billion-dollar fund of which I was Founding Chairman.

Fast forward thirty years and I find myself in Beijing, furthering Calvert's social impact investing program by investing in the first environmental fund in China. I was involved in other projects there to spread the "do well by doing good" consciousness. But the Chinese are very practical and it seemed the Communist Party wanted to be the main fountain of goodness and the government was always suspect of foreign NGOs (non-governmental organizations, like Greenpeace). In fact, except for very strong and admirable family values, the concept of charity is quite recent in China as social responsibility has traditionally been the domain of the government. This is also somewhat true in other parts of the world, including European governments. In the USA, charity and donations to nonprofits are an important part of American society as a form of individual self-expression and being a responsible person in the community.

Well, after much work in China I began to believe the valuable work is in building compassion and consciousness in people. I reflected on how more mindfulness in the world, and especially in China where there is so much stress, might eventually be a key to world peace and individual wellbeing. We opened the second mindfulness/floatation center in Beijing. We started manufacturing float tanks in 2018 and began marketing in 2019.

So the float tank experience both saved my business and also gave me a great way to grow old through the benefits of MBSR (mindfulness based stress reduction). We are having a blast. Most of our clientele are wonderful educated Chinese women under forty. They bring their cautious husbands, many of whom are involved in finance. It is amusing to ask these men if they know of the person who runs the largest hedge fund in the world. They usually do, and I remind them that this guy, Ray Dalio, is always telling people the main key to his success is "meditation." Ah. And we are expanding. My gratitude and love to those float pioneers, Lee and Glenn, who manifested their special compassion that continues to reverberate around the world.

Diary of a Floater
Oz Fritz

My name is Oz Fritz and I have been asked
to write about some of my experiences using the
floatation tank. It is a tool and strategy that I
have been working with consistently for about
thirty years now. I still float daily and find it
just as useful if not more so than when I first started. I am a music
producer and sound engineer by profession, a seeker of the vast
untapped potential of the human nervous system by inclination,
an explorer of the Unknown by habit.

In my opinion, if everyone floated regularly, especially the
leaders and powerful people whose decisions affect all our lives,
things would look much different on our planet: more hopeful and
more aligned with life-sustaining goals that benefit, nourish, and
sustain us all. Perhaps I am an overly optimistic idealist, but it is
hard to deny the clarity of thought engendered in an environment
largely free from external stimulus, i.e. the tank. I do not know if
floating can change the world, but I do know that it changed my
world significantly for the better.

People ask, "What do you do in there?" I have tried all kinds
of things and have experimented with it in a wide variety of ways.
It is certainly not my intention to tell anyone how to use the tank.
I admire John Lilly's cautious approach against trying to program
anyone's tank experience for them. Rather, I offer my experiences
and experiments as a record to show what is possible and what
floating has done in my life.

I began floating at a transitional point in my life when making
a switch from working as a live soundman touring with bar bands
to a recording engineer. I had recently moved to New York City to
increase my chances at getting a job in a recording studio. Though
I had done some recording in the past, and working at live sound
has the same basic goal of trying to make a group sound good, it
still was starting over from scratch. Just getting in the door of a
reputable studio was a challenge. I spent three hours waiting in the
lobby of a top studio called The Hit Factory, the last studio that

John Lennon worked at, only to be told "don't call us, we'll call you." They never did. Finally, I was fortunate to get an internship at an up and coming studio in Greenwich Village. An internship in a recording studio is an unpaid job that involves answering the phone, making coffee, cleaning up and running errands. After three months, I was promoted to assistant engineer, a paid staff position. This is when the real studio education began. Not long after that I had my first float.

I became interested in floating through reading books by John Lilly, particularly *The Center of the Cyclone*. At this point in my life, at the ripe old age of twenty-seven, I had an advanced case, almost an obsession, with consciousness exploration. Floating sounded like a great way to satisfy this vice without having to drop out of life or suffer the physical mortifications of the extreme yogis. I was sure there would be somewhere to float in New York but did not get around to finding a place because I did not feel ready — whatever that meant. It was a catch-22; I was not conscious enough to try a tool that would raise my consciousness, or so I imagined. This changed when I was given a three-float package for my twenty-eighth birthday. I thought, ready or not, I might as well give it a shot.

At that point, I had just been promoted to assistant engineer and was living at the Sivananda Yoga Center on Twenty-fourth Street to save money. The rent was very low, and included an obligation to attend their mediation service held every morning at six o'clock a.m. It started with a half hour of seated, silent meditation which my body found torturous. I never came close to achieving any kind of transcendent experience with this technique beyond being incredibly happy when it was over. My first time in the tank was just about the exact opposite. I could drop the body, let it go and fly off into the realms of meditation, contemplation and introspection with the greatest ease. This was clearly the technique for me.

I also came to see that my hesitancy and nervousness in trying out a floatation tank was the result of a deeply buried, unconscious fear. If you have ever read any of John Lilly's accounts of tank work you know that he has written about some pretty far-out encounters. I was not quite yet ready to go way beyond the Earth game, visit distant sectors of cosmic space, and bump into vast non-human entities; for all I knew, a common occurrence when floating. Believe me, it is not. I also had impressions about the floating experience from seeing the film *Altered States*, an unrealistic, Hollywood drama based on John Lilly's initial research and experiments with isolation. This fear of intense, unknown experiences completely dissipated when Sam Zeiger, my guide for the first voyage, gave a floating orientation prior to my first time. He had me feel how light the tank door was, how easily it opened. "You can get out whenever you like. You can even put a towel in the door to have it be open just a crack if it is too dark." I tried opening the door and it was as light as a feather. My fear of floating immediately disappeared. I have never been afraid to use the tank since.

My audio career took off fairly quickly; it was an exciting time. I would get into the habit of floating every morning before going into the recording session. This made me feel very clear, present and alert. The job of an assistant engineer required staying one step ahead, anticipating what the engineer or producer needed next to keep the studio session flowing smoothly. I noticed my brain functioning faster and more efficiently after floating. It seems that when consciousness moves at a faster rate, time slows down. Another way to put it: it feels like you have more time to get something set up or to make quick technical decisions.

The heightened attention and presence engendered by an hour of sensory attenuation and deep relaxation also proved useful for walking the often dangerous streets of New York in the 1980s. It seems muggers rarely attack people acutely aware of what is going on around them. They like to get the jump on people lost in their thoughts and not paying attention. I moved to Clinton Street in the southeast corner of the Lower East Side and would occasionally have to walk home at two am or later, crossing through terrain of abandoned urban decay populated by drug addicts and homeless people off their meds and their rockers. I would navigate this territory with all the intense awareness of going through a war zone and never had a problem.

Over time, I discovered that the deep relaxation and tranquility from floating was not only cumulative but stays with the body as an enduring state of mind even in circumstances of great stress. There seemed no shortage of stress in the upper echelons of the music industry back then. Platinum Island, the studio where I worked, would get visits from Tommy Mottola, the head of Sony, and his young wife Mariah Carey, a rising star at the time. Madonna would drop by, Meat Loaf, Iggy Pop and the Ramones all recorded or mixed there. The combination of expensive studios and artist egos putting themselves on the line was guaranteed to provoke stress in all the staff attempting to keep everyone happy. Deep underneath the surface turmoil, I felt a layer of calm that helped maintain a clear perspective and avoid overwhelm. This layer of calm detachment increased and became more stable through frequent floating.

Creative visualization was an excellent tool that produced greater results when practiced in the tank. The next big leap up the ladder of a technician in the music business was going from a staff engineer/assistant engineer to an independent, freelance engineer. When on staff at a busy commercial studio, you are always assured of getting regular work. As a freelance engineer, though you typically make more money, you have to find your own clients. You are no longer supported by the shingle of the studio where you once had employment. I experimented with techniques from *Creative Visualization* by Shakti Gawain. Soon, I adopted those methods for use in the tank. When the studio schedule looked sparse, I would go through some steps to getting very deeply relaxed in the tank then visualize myself in the studio engineering sessions. It seemed to work, only it started working too well. I would get offers for amazing projects with conflicting schedules, so I would have to choose. This does not seem like a bad problem to have, nevertheless I did stop visualizing session work opting for the more natural methods of chance and coincidence control. I have been cautious about using creative visualization ever since. The old adage proves true: be careful what you ask for because you just might get it... and then some.

Sam Zeiger, the owner/operator of Blue Light floatation on Twenty-third Street in New York where I initially floated, and I became friends. After my hour-long sessions, he would serve refreshing herbal tea and we would discuss subjects ranging from philosophy and metaphysics to the chances of the Mets making the play-offs. It was Sam who sold me my first tank, his old one, when he upgraded. That was in 1988 and I have never been without one since. Sam, another inveterate researcher into consciousness exploration, also introduced me to the work of E.J. Gold and his community, the Institute for the Development of the Harmonious Human Being.

I first came across E.J. Gold's *American Book of the Dead* (ABD) when Bill Laswell brought a copy into the studio after one of his frequent shopping trips to the incredible bookstores New York boasted at the time. Not long after that, Sam showed me its practical use, to deliver instructions to the soul or being (called the Voyager) of the recently deceased. I began doing readings and found it an excellent meditation practice. Attempting to make contact with a non-biological form of life, the consciousness of the deceased, seemed to forge new tracks into the territory of inner space.

I had been experimenting with rituals and exercises using a death/rebirth formula for some time, and it seemed natural to bring that work into the tank. They helped accelerate a path of brain-change leading toward transformation. I would simulate my own death in the tank and journey through an after-life leading to rebirth using an exercise from Aleister Crowley. After going through the practice of Labyrinth readings for a few months, I enlisted a partner to read to me from the ABD while I simulated the experience of death in the tank. I had a microphone connected to speakers at the time, but it can also be read through the tank door. Although I had delivered these instructions more than once and had some familiarity with them, the random chamber chosen to read was right there with me in my death shroud, exactly what I needed to hear at that moment, quite uncanny and hard to describe. I had not ever been on the other end of a reading until simulating death in the tank.

When I had the time, I would see how long I could float. There were a few five- and six-hour sessions and one or two that went just over seven. The muscles would start to get sore from not moving. I do not remember many dramatic changes on the conscious level except one instance. Before floating, I had been reading *Finnegans Wake* by James Joyce for the first time, understanding very little of it. After an extended period in the tank I experienced a breakthrough where I could almost see multiple meanings in everything I encountered, all existing simultaneously at different points in space. Multiple paths, in the mind's eye, sprang up from every encounter.

I do not miss floating when I am unable to do so, from traveling, or recently from moving...until I get back into the tank and reconnect with the space that is connected to everything else.

Revival Inspiration
Heather McNeilly

I had never heard of floating before my first time. A friend sent me a picture and told me "we should try this." I went to visit my grandmother in San Francisco shortly thereafter and booked an appointment at a float spa there. I had read about the benefits and had suffered with back pain and migraines for years. I walked into the float for pain relief, but got so much more. They say it takes a few times for some people to "get it" or to "settle in" to a float. It took me about fifteen minutes in a Samadhi tank. For the first fifteen minutes (or so…time is definitely hard to grasp in there) I had anxiety…imagining an earthquake, imagining the tank door would not open…continually having to remind myself to think positive thoughts.

The woman at the front desk had told me "You may drift off to sleep. If that happens we will come and gently knock on the door to wake you when your time is up." I laughed to myself, certain this would never happen. My heart was racing too fast; there would be no drifting off to anywhere for me. And then…the next thing I know…this same woman is having to knock on my door to wake me.

I walked out of that spa forever changed. I felt like I was walking on clouds for days after that first float. I would try and describe my experience to everyone I came in contact with, but I would fail because I struggled to find words to describe the amazing floatiness that had not left me. I was hooked. I found the closest float center to my home, which was about a forty-five-minute drive. I went often. The more I went the more I dreamed of sharing this with everyone.

I live in Grass Valley, a small, beautiful town in the Sierra Foothills. I felt like this business would be good here but did not think I could do it on my own. I had some friends (Antonio and Jacqueline Lucero) that kept talking about starting a business in town. Over the years I mentioned floating to them and they mentioned wanting to start a wellness business. As the years went by I continued to float and fall deeper in love with everything about it. I could not shake the desire that I wanted to do this. I felt passion. Floating was changing my life. I wanted to share that passion. And my heart told me that Antonio and Jaqueline were the right ones to do it with.

After one particular float I walked to a nearby coffee shop and started making notes and writing numbers on a napkin, and sent a message: "I think we can actually make this work." I explained that either I was loopy from the float, or I really thought we could do this. The message that I received back was simple: "Come over. Let's sit down and talk." And I did. And we did. We started right then and there. We wrote business plans and pros and cons and dreamed and drew and added and subtracted. We never stopped from that moment. Antonio was a force to be reckoned with. Once he wanted something – he went full speed ahead to get it. Jackie was the reason. She brought us down to earth with the "what if's" that we definitely needed to consider. And I was the dreamer. This was my dream, and I wanted it more than anyone knew. They believed in me, and I believed in them. We opened the doors to Revival Float & Wellness on December 6, 2016, two years after sitting down for that first meeting. All three of us have second businesses, so we had to work day and night to make this come true.

We had no idea how our community would respond. We held our breath and crossed all our fingers and toes. Not only has our community embraced us in so many beautiful and unexpected ways, we continue to feel like we are the ones receiving instead of providing. The healing that is happening constantly stops us in our tracks and brings tears to our eyes. In the two and a half years that we have been open we have witnessed so many amazing moments. Transformative moments. People have walked in carrying enormous amounts of pain, both physical and emotional, and we have gotten to watch them walk out lighter and freer.

I have floated more than I ever imagined I would be able to. I did thirty days in a row the first year we were open, tracking numbers with a doctor, and seeing firsthand how this can impact your health in so many beneficial ways. During the second year I floated for one hundred one days in a row, and I watched my own life change in ways that I struggle to put into words. Jackie floated during her entire pregnancy and we all got to watch her have the best, most blissful pregnancy we had seen. We cry regularly simply from pure joy. To get to watch people heal and transform before your eyes is a beautiful, beautiful thing. To get to share this dream with so many people is, itself, a dream come true.

Cami's Twins
Cambelle Logan

Floating while pregnant offered a precious unwinding. Because I was carrying twins I had a deep apprehension about my birth scenario. The relaxed home birth I had wanted was no longer an option, and my new reality was filled with frequent monitoring and testing. Floating gave me a chance to drop into my body, and into something deeper than the physical. It gave me a chance to slip into the liminal, where psychic communication can occur between a mother and the babes in her womb.

I floated several times in the couple of months leading up to my birth. I quieted my mind and communicated with my babies' spirits, enlisting their help in a smooth transition earthside. I was able to release a lot of my fear, knowing we were a team. Floating helped me create the space within myself to have this communication. One day I floated, and I knew I would give birth very soon. At that point I was enormous and the buoyant quality of the water felt divine. I tapped into my inner lightness

and surrendered. That day was a Thursday, and I gave birth Sunday evening to two beautiful healthy children.

Expanding My Outlook
Bryan Bennett

During my college years at Georgia Tech (four decades ago), I met and became friends with students from India and southeast Asia who were Hindus and Buddhists. Out of curiosity, I often discussed with these individuals their meditation and spiritual experiences, and I read their religious books (the *Bhagavad Gita*, the *Upanishads,* the *Dhammapada*, the *Bardo Thodol*, the various Sutras, etc.). I found the spirituality described in these books and the descriptions of unusual meditation experiences recounted by these individuals to be inspiring and fascinating. This in turn led me to an interest in meditation and eventually to lucid dreaming. I have found lucid dreams to be extraordinarily wonderful and supra-mundane experiences, but unfortunately too rare in occurrence and too short in duration.

Not long after graduating, I read Richard Feynman's wonderful book, *Surely You're Joking, Mr. Feynman!* in which he describes his experiences in the isolation tank of John Lilly. Having taken many classes in physics while attending college, I found my professors of physics to be very candid individuals, and so I was rather inclined to believe what Feynman described of his experiences in Lilly's isolation tanks. Consequently, I was extremely interested at that point in floating and I soon discovered the Samadhi Tank company.

I purchased and began floating in my Samadhi tank in the fall of 1998. At first, I found the floatation experience to be fantastically relaxing (especially after a physically vigorous day since my job frequently required long distance walking). As a result, I would often fall into a deep sleep, but just prior to that, I would experience the most vivid and realistic hypnagogic images that I ever had. Those images would frequently persist far longer than the hypnagogic images that I experienced while falling asleep in bed.

Eventually, after a couple of years, I began to have experiences that would understandably provoke incredulity in most people. I will attempt to describe one such unusual experience here. Sometimes (and on rare occasions), I awakened from a deep sleep in my Samadhi tank to an experience of acoustic and somatic waves, simultaneously hearing and feeling the vibrations. It was like nothing that I had previously experienced, but it was definitely not uncomfortable or painful. At that point, I discovered that I was able to "project" my awareness outside of my physical body. I then noticed that I had no arms or legs, or any awareness of my physical body whatsoever, but I was as mentally lucid as I ever was during waking consciousness. Also, the lucidity in that experience and its prolonged duration were much more easily maintained than the lucidity in, or duration of, my lucid dreams. This inclined me to believe that this experience might be fundamentally different from dreaming, whether lucid or non-lucid, but of course I cannot definitively say for certain.

There were eventually other experiences even more unusual than what I described above, but they were also very rare. What is not rare is the deep and refreshing relaxation that I have found while floating in my Samadhi tank and the expanded outlook on our "reality" that those floatation experiences have provided me.

My Journey in Search of Consciousness
Walburga Ziegenhagen

To submerge myself in the warmth and darkness of the salt solution of a floatation tank, my body held in a safe embrace, freeing up my mind to travel, is one of the greatest adventures I have so far experienced.

My first involvement with the Samadhi Tank Company was working in their office. I was eight months pregnant and had just arrived in the area for a one-year stay. Lee and Glenn organized a floating experience for my husband and me, and, I have to admit, for me was not one of those big "I will never forget" moments.

Upon my return to Germany I insisted on getting my own tank. We lived in a big apartment in Cologne with a nice little room for the tank and built a big bed around and on top of it. In my first floating sessions I mainly dealt with the sensation of panic in closed and dark rooms, claustrophobia, I was carrying around since my childhood. Just looking at the tank in my own home brought up the fearful remembrance of anxiety. Nevertheless, I had bought a tank. My determination to be able to float and my curiosity were stronger than my conditioned expectation. I was determined to figure out a way to trick myself into a better experience.

I started out with the door open, floating with my head towards the door. I was able to look out, see the light and feel the air coming in, not the most enjoyable floating experience because it was too cold in the tank and way too bright. The next step was putting a towel between the door and the door frame, leaving the door just a crack open. Still I could see some light but I had reduced the draft and fresh air was entering the tank. During that process I realized that it was actually not the darkness or the closed, small room, which made me freak out, it was the airflow. The picture of the dark, closed, and small room produced a sensation in my lungs. Warm, humid, stagnant, heavy air was the picture of oppression.

Still I was not satisfied with my floating posture. I knew how people were floating and I was eager to do it the right way. Real floaters had their head to the back. So, my next step was shifting my head from the front to the back of the tank while still having the door a crack open with my towel. I still could feel the draft of cold air disturbing the surface of my body. Finally, I let go even of the towel holding the door open. To my utter relief, with my head close to the back of the tank, I could feel air flowing into the tank through a vent opening, there by design. The sensation of coolness calmed my senses. It was just enough to be picked up by my nostrils, but not enough to create a disturbing feeling. In the early tanks the ventilation was created by a fan box that had a slight hum. It was a big relief to hear that hum signifying air flow. I felt successful and content.

After ten years in Germany my family and I came back to California. I was living with internal turmoil. My irritating and confusing thoughts about me, about other people and about my environment were so predominant that they were sabotaging my life. I could see that I was not acting in real time, driven by inner assumptions about people, about life, about what was happening around me, assumptions that came out of a pool of my past life. Old memories were surfacing, leaving no space for the experience of real time.

Glenn suggested that I start floating every day for a while and I began a daily routine of waking up and using the tank first thing, at five o'clock a.m. The regular floating helped to minimize my thought overload. I did not solve any of my problems while I was floating, but my nerve system calmed way down. I made a connection to my body through hearing my own heartbeat. At times it felt like a shamanic drum pounding along in a steady rhythm with the sole purpose to remind me, this is you being here. I fully enjoyed being in the tank, a place of my own, where I could be alone with myself. This all contributed to the healing of my mind and brought me back to real time, in the here and now. Getting out of the tank I felt calm and at ease. In the early morning hours, opening the tank room, going out into nature was a blissful moment—everything crisp and clear. I could hear better and see more.

After a series of enjoyable floats it felt like my mind was getting bored. The mind does not like having to play second violin, giving room to nice body experiences and not the dominant part leading human behavior. So my mind decided to get busy again. All of a sudden all different sorts of scenarios were flashing: what will happen if the power goes out, or if somebody is coming into the room and opening the tank door, the pump could go on while I am still floating, there could be an earthquake outside and the tank will collapse on top of me... My body went haywire with these catastrophic scenarios in my mind. My heart started beating like crazy, my breathing got flat and excited, my whole body was screaming "Get me out of here." In no time I was out of the tank and gasping for air. Clearly my mind was triggering my body sensations.

With this insight I carefully began to watch my thoughts while floating. If I would notice the slightest notion of a disturbing thought coming up in my mind, I would immediately look at it and start arguing with it, reasoning myself into the fact that everything was fine, that I was safe. Or I created ways in my mind of responding to possible disastrous situations. After a while I got tired of doing these brain acrobatics. I began to not take those attention calling thoughts of my mind seriously. Why should I listen to my mind? When thoughts or pictures came up I would try letting them go away again. I experienced that I could handle them, that they just were figments of my imagination. I learned a lot about myself, my psyche, my thoughts and my body. How my thoughts influence my body, how my body influences my thoughts and that there is something else behind all that constant drama.

The second phase started after I was able to really relax into the float experience to the point that the body was nice and content and the mind could go on its own way, doing what it likes to do, coming up with stuff, does not matter if important or not. Then I began to feel the separation of the mind and the body, a drifting apart of those two members, very similar to when I was falling asleep, but in this case I was not asleep. There was still an awareness of the body in the warm, dark and wet surrounding on the one hand and the active mind on the other, which was

236

separated from the body, drifting upwards, at least in my mind's eye.

At this point in my floating, I never had practiced any form of meditation and did not know how similar the two experiences can be. I was surprised by the multitude of scenarios unfolding in front of me, maybe even universes. Sometimes it felt very strange to be seeing things without any reference point to my own life, so much that I often felt bewildered by them, just an observer of strange things passing through my mind. Then more and more something seemed to pull my mind further out, or maybe further away from my body, resulting in me feeling far out there somewhere and, now, all of a sudden I had to deal with coming back into my body, another task I first did not know how to handle.

The same conditions I had encountered in the beginning of my float journey showed now up again. The moment my conscious mind was entering my body, a feeling of claustrophobia, of "man, this body feels way too small for me", started to arise. It was almost like an incarnation experience. When the mind enters the body it has to deal with the smallness of human existence. I understood that a big issue for me is transitions, the disruption caused to my system of moving from one place to another.

All those things I had learned in the beginning of my float journey I could again apply to this semi new situation, perhaps experiencing myself, both the same and different, happening on a higher level, one spiral round up. There was another round of staying with the sensations of my body, calming them through intentional breathing and using observation of my mind to mold the experience into a blissful one. Then, getting so tired of the whole effort to keep things in line, I realized it was a matter of just letting things come up, not clinging to them, maintaining an unbiased attitude of neither attracted nor repelled. This meant giving the things no significance, not making them big and threatening to my system. Just letting them show up on the stage of my mind and then letting them leave the stage again, while I am just the observer, enjoying my own theater in all its magnificence.

I began to look forward to this challenge/adventure every time I floated. I do not want to imply that I have mastered this process, or even that I am able to apply it to my own life. But I did get a glimpse of how my mind functions and where I get hung up in the whole process so much that I sabotage the ease of my own life experience.

I am very grateful for the people who have created the Samadhi Floatation Tank. I hope that in the future more people will use this tool to explore their own minds.

APPENDIX

Common Ground
Jason McDonald

It has been my pleasure to get to know members of the international float community and work alongside them as their industry has grown in recent years. One truth I have come to know in my years as a Public Health Inspector is that for the relationship between an industry and health officials to be successful, it is vital to establish common ground. The common ground I have found with the floatation industry is agreement that "health is good for business." I want safe outcomes, and so does the industry.

Part of what has enchanted me in working with the floatation industry has been seeing the commitment from industry members to provide safe, healthy, enjoyable and (sometimes) life-altering experiences. The other rewarding aspect has been the opportunity to explore a part of public health that has, to date, been relatively undiscovered. When new activities emerge, like floatation has, we public health officials feel compelled to proactively make sure health is protected. In other words, we try to take steps to prevent injury or illness before they occur. These precautionary actions can take the form of education, health promotion, regulation and enforcement.

Public Health Inspectors are very familiar with swimming pool environments. Swimming is one of the best forms of physical exercise that a person can do. However, because of well-documented incidences of injury, illness, infection and even death associated with pools and spas, our attention is naturally drawn to any form of recreational water activity. To no one's surprise, health officials are curious about floatation and interested in finding the best ways to protect the public. Perhaps because water is wet, some naturally want to utilize their pool expertise and local pool regulations to help assess risks with floatation.

I suppose I know a little bit about swimming pools. I am the provincial policy lead on aquatics for our government and

240

have inspected hundreds of pools and hot tubs of all shapes and sizes, from the decks to the mechanical rooms. It has been my strong opinion from day one that meditating in float solution is nothing like swimming. Relaxing in a hot tub is not comparable to floating. For me, floatation shares more differences than similarities with swimming pool and spa use. I concede that others disagree with me on this, but they are entitled to be incorrect.

The unintended consequence of health officials approaching floatation tanks in the same manner as pools and spas is that floatation gets unnecessarily miscast as a risky practice. In reality, the likelihood of seeing the types and rates of infections and injuries typically associated with pools and spas is infinitesimal. To their credit, the floatation industry has established a strong capacity to articulate how floatation is different from swimming in recent years. Industry knowledge and advocacy in this regard has helped to better frame the risk assessments that health officials and regulators perform.

Business owners and health officials alike should know the important distinctions between floating and swimming. They include:

- Even before float solution is filtered and treated, the epsom salt level creates an inhospitable growth environment for microorganisms.
- Due to the face-up position of the body, the inactive nature of floating and the noticeable salt taste, float tank solution is far less likely to be inadvertently swallowed than when swimming or wading. For the kinds of recreational water illnesses that we typically worry about to occur, one needs to first swallow the water.
- Floatation is typically limited to one person at a time, or to couples who very likely know one another intimately. Float tanks are safer simply because far fewer patrons use them at any given time and over the course of a day.
- Unlike outdoor pools and spas, floatation occurs in controlled indoor environments with separation from outside sources of contamination.
- Floatation involves an older, more mature, client profile.

Children, who are known polluters of public pools, rarely if ever use floatation tanks.

- Fecal, blood and vomit accidents are more likely to be detected and remedied in a floatation setting because user entry and exit is more controlled by staff than in pool and spa environments.
- Fouling of the solution by sweat is not of concern like it is in swimming pools and spas as float solution is purposely kept the same as skin temperature and the user lies static.
- Float facilities typically offer one-to-one instruction and dialogue with every new floater, whereas pool facilities passively rely on signage to communicate health and safety messaging. Face to face instruction empowers floaters to be more aware of, and committed to observing, safe procedures.
- Floaters are more likely to shower prior to floatation than users of pools and spas, meaning less germs are carried in. Additionally, because the epsom salt clings to the skin of the floater, users typically shower to remove it. This reduces the number of germs that might adhere to skin.
- Circulation is disengaged during floatation, significantly lowering risks of entrapment, evisceration, disembowelment or drowning attributed to pool and spa suction outlets.

I am not trying to convince anyone that floatation tanks do not present some inherent hazards to their users. It is not like float studio owners can just fill a tank, walk away and watch the money pile up. I have personally tested float tank solution and found Pseudomonas. I have felt how slippery the float solution can make a surface. Anytime there is water near electricity, there are potential electrical hazards.

My feeling is that the existence of potential hazards in a floatation environment does not make floatation risky. Just because float tanks have suction outlets does not mean that children are going to be disemboweled like they have been in pools. Just because a floatation tank may test positive for Pseudomonas, does not necessarily mean it needs to be closed. Just because float solutions contain water does not mean that floatation tanks require lifeguards.

242

Health officials, myself included, can do better than feeling like we are best protecting public health by having floatation conform to existing swimming pool standards. We have to see and believe in floatation as a non-drug approach to improving the physical and psychological well-being of the public. I personally feel that if one person who needs floatation misses their opportunity, it eventually leads to an increased burden of some kind to the health care system. Miscasting floatation as risky can stifle the industry and unnecessarily close tanks and businesses. By working together, the floatation industry and health officials can continue to develop appropriate minimum standards and observe more and more of the safe outcomes we currently see across North America.

Closing Remarks Float Con 2020, Virtual Edition
Stephen W. Johnson

In a time of division, confusion, rancor and pain, how can we not believe in the culture changing aspect of the Float; to be aware of how forces could come to bear, to control this deeply effective therapeutic, awareness enhancing experience and practice. For through this experience we achieve a deeper seeing. Maybe from an essence, through the inner to the outer. Could that essence be of a wisdom which must go through a process to manifest in physical reality, to manifest in our lives. Through the Float, does not enhancement become more natural?

Is the Float not a wisdom practice? If so, that heightened, broadened awareness would evidence as a healing practice, maybe a spiritual practice, which we are beginning to see via our researchers, thinkers, writers, explorers, and that we have always felt in the Float. A felt sense of connection, of relationality, of being "of." A philosopher calls it becoming the "cosmic citizen." We know, in our minds and hearts, our experience, through our contemplative and wisdom practices, that ecological and ontological grounding are vital, as well as intertwined. In a way, they are a grounding in a protean, creative, fluid state which is rich in possibility and change. Do we not immerse in such a state in the Float? Do we not become witness to wonder?

It is not the world that needs saving, we do. We are multiple, diversities, complexities. We are a living, experiencing intersection. We are the jewels in Indra's Net. We are defined by creativity, originality, fervid life. We are process. We are suspended in an erotic of existence. We live in an imbricated, layered reality of constant change, being and becoming. Through our practice, through the Float, we can become conscious of and open to those multiple realities. Not just personal, psychological realities but of the other and the other-than-human; the transpersonal, the spiritual, which refuse to be defined and controlled by a dominating culture.

I suggest that we, in this community, are the purveyors, gate-keepers, practitioners and educators of an experience that is fundamentally about freedom. The freedom of becomings, of change, the freedom inherent in the enhancement of perception and awareness. The freedom in our natural intertwining tendency, and henceforth about compassion, creativity, kindness and, yes, Love.

This makes this a radical act, and we as activists of how the ecological and psychological are wed. Activists of the communion of science and spirit. The scientific is essential to the evolution of consciousness and our complex, troubled world. But, so is the spiritual. We have and continue to hear and be given updates of research being done related to the Float, and thus far, it has been spectacular. It is with huge gratitude that we listen and acknowledge this essential work. But, what of the spiritual, which escapes easy articulation and current methodology? The Float was created, in part, for the exploration and enhancement of consciousness and as a contemplative and spirit practice.

I would like to briefly look at two words/concepts that are related to the float, and have been used peripherally toward the spirit, the contemplative. The Nothing and The Void. For The Nothing I will quote the great Portland writer Lidia Yuknavitch, "Let the top of your head lift, see? There are spaces between things…What you thought was nothingness carries the life…" The Void, in spiritual literature and in many creation myths, denotes the Tehom, the deep saltwater chaos. "How everything begins in darkness" (Catherine Keller), The Void as the mystical concept of the "Plenum/Void" where the supposed nothing is the pre-state of the all. The Void as generative essence, chaotic substrate and how it relates to creativity and becomings, the state where all possibility exists pre-definition. The Nothing, The Void as symbol space, spirit space. Is this not the space we enter in the float?

The ease, the depth and the uniqueness of the Float, position it as, possibly, the most effective practice to help facilitate the communion of science and spirit.

An Interview with E.J. Gold
for the 2014 Float Conference
Glenn Perry & Lee Perry

GP: So I am going to talk to you for a minute about E.J. (EJ) Gold. John Lilly introduced EJ to Lee and me, and, when we moved to Grass Valley, he became a teacher, friend and neighbor. He has had numerous versions of our tanks at different times over the years. He is an American artist, author, musician and spiritual teacher. EJ's large-scale jazz art paintings have served as backdrops for Herbie Hancock, Wynton Marsalis, Nancy Wilson, Oscar Peterson, and Jazz at Lincoln Center performances. He has written and self-published over fifty books including the 1970s classic, *American Book of the Dead.* He is the founder of the Institute for the Development of the Harmonious Human Being.

He has, for many years, acted as an independent spiritual teacher whose work and style bear a strong affinity with the teachings of Gurdjieff and the Fourth Way school of thought, as well as Tibetan and Zen Buddhism, Jewish Kabbalah, and Christian mysticism. Like with Gurdjieff, the fundamental emphasis of Gold's teaching is on the concept of spiritual work in daily life with a constant effort to increase and maintain heightened awareness in all activities.

He is also a hilarious stand-up comic. He was invited to present at this Conference by Float On. He does not travel and so was asked to send a digital recording. He invited us over to find out about the conference and the following is what happened.

EJ: So I kind of let that thing, you know, lie there. So I will tell you a story about John that I thought was very funny comedy. First of all, he called because he was very excited that you guys had come up with something that did not drip, just did not drip ever. This is after the Japanese, that Japanese bizarre disaster tank.

GP: Yes, the Samadhi Tube.

EJ: It was a fiberglass Samadhi tank. Yes, total disaster. Right after that you guys built one that was fabulous, and that is the one that I have experienced. And the UFO was behind that. The best part of it was that it did not impinge upon my body. It did not remind me that I had a body and that it was there in this tank and so on. The faster, to me, the tank gets out of the way, the better the tank is, and that is exactly why I actually started with and kept with the Samadhi tank in spite of the fact that I know you guys as well as I did.

This gets the body out of the way like twenty years of meditation would do, but here you get into the tank and nothing bad is going to happen to you in the tank. First of all, that is a very good thing to know. Nothing bad will happen to you in the tank, no. I am sitting there going, "Oh wait a minute it is dark it is…," you know the temperature was not right for me, I like a nice warm bath. It was cool. I got used to that. It was okay, and then there was this mind-boggling thing that was just driving me crazy, waiting for the drip and nothing and so...

LP: You cannot be satisfied.

EJ: No, it is true. I saw it as an escape velocity, as a way of getting out, off the planet very easily because it does two things. Two wonderful things. One is it isolates you from the environment and gives you a safe environment within that. It is a bubble, it is a great bubble, a safety bubble. And secondly, most importantly, it takes gravity off, it takes those six miles, that six-mile-high column of air off of you momentarily. And gives you freedom from gravity. Not complete freedom but certainly a lot of freedom from gravity. Enough that it can set you into orbit almost immediately.

And as you get acclimated to the tank, you know this. The folks maybe will not necessarily know this. It takes a while to get acclimated to the tank, duh. You start out working in a gymnasium, and you do not get results the first day. Come on, do not be a nut, you were not going to get results the first twenty seconds you are doing anything. So you get used to the tank, acclimatized to the tank, you start bonding. This is no joke, no, you start bonding. I work with bonding all the time. I work with bonding with animals all the time. I work with bonding with Feng Shui spaces all the time. I work with fountains all the time. Bonding is an issue, always is. Whether you know it or not you are getting into a relationship which is going to last years, maybe your whole lifetime. That can be a plant that you brought into your house; it is certainly going to be something you get so intimate with that you get inside it for hours at a time. In order to be able to reveal to yourself your innermost... well, we will get to that in a second, right?

This is where I went with it; a lot of people use this just to chill. This is very cool, and chilling is good. They also use the things for relief of chronic ailments and illnesses and pains and aches and miseries and so forth, and that is also very, very good. You just zero out the body by getting into the tank and acclimating yourself to it. Learning how to do that takes a few times, right?

GP: Yes.

EJ: An individual can get into a tank and eliminate twenty years of learning how to zero out the body. I am in the tank right now.

LP: Are you?

EJ: Oh yes, and in the tank, I am the tank. I am one with the tank, and you only learn that by actually experiencing getting into the tank; having it happen. Yo, hey, that was kind of fun, uh, sort of... I have had, you know, funner times. This was very enlightening to say the least, and eventually you will be enlightened. In other words, the point of the process of enlightenment is to get lighter, no? Seriously. I mean that is seriously true. And to relieve oneself of the burden of the body and the burden of the mind; no faster way to do that.

Now in the tank, one thing that can happen in the tank, I was going to tell you, happened to one of the guys who was doing a tank trip. On the previous day he had gotten out of the tank and showered. You had the shower afterwards to get the salt off.

GP: Right.

EJ: Still have to do that, right?

GP: Yeah.

EJ: Yeah, that has not changed. So the technology is really pretty much the same.

LP: Yeah, we are trying to keep it just like that.

EJ: Yes, so, and you perfect small things rather than big things. You perfect small things. It is just so everything works and it stays working. You do not throw one thing out. Because you can do that with improvements, you can throw other things out of whack with an improvement, as engineers know.

So then this guy I was doing this with, he was showering, he got out, he showered, he drove home in a beautiful Maserati. I think you know who I am talking about. He had a beautiful Maserati, and he drove this bomb home. And he woke up in the tank. He had been in how many? Three times is it? You know the story. It was the third time, right? This happened?

GP: I did it too.

EJ: And you did it too?

LP: Not in a Maserati though.

EJ: No, but he did the same thing. And the first time that I tried that I did not. But on my fifth tank experience, I did experience that double looping. What happens is, you get a time loop out of the thing and you start projecting a full-blown tactile hallucination similar to the way that the earth is... or the way the universe is produced. It is a full-blown tactile hallucination, too. When you are meditating in that space, it becomes an amazing tool, and that is what I have found is a transformational tool. It is just unsurpassed. There is nothing like it on this planet.

There is a very, very high level, and this I agree with, a very high level of selfness that creates what one is. That is the character builder that builds your character, that makes your character do what your character does, sets your character up, basically chooses, selects the character's traits. That goes very well with the Buddhist concept that your tendencies are you; your tendencies, the things that you are likely to do, and you are likely to do again.

One of the things that I am hoping that somebody will do is combine some of my inductions like the relaxation induction, things like that, with the tank, and see what happens with people, how people respond to that. I think that would be very exciting because I think that being led through a series of inducted journeys would help people. Also, there are extra-dimensional journeys as well that I have set up. I think that would go well with the tank although I do not know anybody who is experimenting with that at this time. It is just started. I just released those things so it has only been weeks, so we have not had any feedback on it. But that would be kind of a fun thing to see if anybody can use those for that purpose, particularly to do the meta- programming. And I do have inductions that are meta-programming inductions of course.

LP: Okay.

EJ: I have a good time with the Epsom salt. It is magnesium sulphate that bothers me.

LP: An "in" joke.

EJ: An "in" joke. It is not true, magnesium sulphate does not bother me nor does $MgSO_4$. I had a friend, he was this friend, he is no more, for what he thought was H_2O was H_2SO_4. Lie in an epsom salt bath for one hour, you will feel great, and then on top of that in a safe environment where you can completely relax, completely let go. This, the other thing, too, that I find very good is that in that environment, because you built it as a safe environment, you can sit up quickly, get out of there fast. You have escape things and all kinds of panic things built in which is fantastic. And many of the tanks do not ever put those panic things in the way you did. To let somebody freak out and get out of there quickly, that is a relief. You know you feel safe because you know you can do that at any time.

And in fact, Toni told me, "Panic," when I was in there. She said, "Panic." And I said, "I shouldn't." Then she said, "No, panic." "Okay, okay, I'll panic." I started groping around, the thing came open really easily, and it popped out. No big deal. Hardly any weight to it, gee, and I am out of the tank. "Alright, now get back into the tank again and now panic again." So yes, panic drill, and so then you feel completely safe. If you have done three panic drills, you feel safe in there forever, no problem. Cause you know you can get out if you need to.

One of the things I appreciated was the fact that it is a safe environment. It feels safe in there. And you can breathe in there, it is very important to be able to breathe. I love to breathe. Yeah, I am so addicted to oxygen I cannot tell you. The doctor that birthed me was in on the conspiracy. He spanked me to get me to breathe this crap, and I have not been able to stop since. Someday I will beat it. But you know, until that day...

GP: That will be the last thing you do.

EJ: Yeah, really, I will beat this oxygen addiction if it is the last thing... I like that as a t-shirt. So the engineering is amazing. I have watched Glenn as an engineer, I, as a fellow engineer, I have watched him engineer and craft these things and come up with solutions. You do not have any idea what has to go into a tank in order to make the thing. You think, "Oh, do you just stamp the things, put them together." Not true right?

GP: There is a little more to it than that.

EJ: Yes, a little more than that. How about a lot more? Everything has to be engineered down to a micron, it really does. And to make it work consistently forever without having to fly out there and fix it for you. Nobody wants to do that, or have you ship it back, God forbid, and then you fix one nut and then you send it back out again. But hey, you have to design so that does not happen; so you do not have those things happen, or as few times as possible. Inevitably something will, now and again. What else do you need to know?

GP: One thing I find is I still have to stretch my face to get really relaxed.

EJ: I thought you were going to say to get it over the skull.

GP: That is good.

EJ: Seems most of the bugs I know have that same problem.

GP: But once I do get it all stretched, it is like I am able to get more into the being space. It seems like I have to get out of the personality.

EJ: Yeah, that is why I recommend the inductions, and because they can help you, guide you, lead you out of the "I am me" and into the "I am all." But it is in stages. It is easy stages, and you can go as far as you want with it. And one of the things you are in the forefront of, something you do not even know what it is yet: "extra dimensional," XD technology, XDT is coming. Know it or not, like it or not, want it or not, it is coming. Because "extra dimensional" is how you actually travel in space. You do not travel by going from one thing in space to another. You travel by going outside and coming back in again. There are machines, devices that can be built to do just exactly that. There are other civilizations,

civilizations that are billions of years older than this civilization. Billions of years, and they still exist. They are still in existence.

Anyway, that tank is a life changer. It is a wonderful experience, and the centers are doing a great deal to, well, "bring the Word of God to the heathen." You know what I mean?

LP: Write that down.

EJ: Yeah, that is as good as..: And do not forget, in the realm of the mind there are no limits.

Will Griffin and Shari Vandervelde Open A Centre
Shari Vandervelde

Will had a ritual when visiting a favorite bookshop. He would descend to the second hand department in the basement, and browse the shelves, pulling out titles which spoke to him in some way. Then he would winnow that armful down to budget. Usually he would read the back, browse the contents, flick through the pages to decide whether it would make the cut. But occasionally there would be one which was a definite must-buy from the moment he saw it. *The Centre of the Cyclone* by John C. Lilly was one such book.

He found the contents fascinating, and quickly devoured it. A few days later he was at a party in London, telling everyone about floatation, and how he wished he could find a tank to try it. Then he emerged into the dawn light to see, just across the road: Floatworks. The hairs rose on the back of his neck—what a weird coincidence.

Years later, during a float, of course, the idea of running a float centre came. But he dismissed it as unrealistic. Over the years the idea would return, each time surrounded by synchronicity, but the rational mind would dismiss it.

More recently Will began to do work which opened him to these communications from the universe, and he began to act on them rather than dismiss them. The universe seemed to notice. Soon enough it became clear that coincidence control was at play, and thanks to the agency of a mutual friend, Will and I found ourselves staying in a tent next to Lee and Glenn Perry's house.

Will said: "We thought we were seeking advice on the mechanics of running a float centre, but the most precious pearl that Lee and Glenn shared with us was infinitely more valuable and practical: how to be with those who come to float." Their insights into how to support the floater and facilitate their experience without imposing our own programs upon them informed not only our behaviour in the float centre, but also its physical layout and design.

We are very grateful to Lee and Glenn, and of course John Lilly. We are also grateful to cosmic coincidence control without the help of which, our centre, Float in the Forest, would not have arisen. There were certainly a lot of challenges during the adventure of opening the float centre, not least the search for a location in the Forest of Dean, in the UK. After the fifteenth fell through, and when it seemed like the barriers were insurmountable, invoking and surrendering to cosmic coincidence control preceded our finding the ideal place. Perhaps, like all those who run float centres, it would appear that we are its agents, and although we may have been unwitting at first, now we embrace it!

A Fond Memory
Gary M. Lee

Greetings Lee,
Oh so very long ago & far away
(somewhere around the early/mid
1970s?) as an inventor, I was designing/
creating custom OEM aquarium filters
in the Hollywood, California area.

One day, while picking up parts
at Ryan Herco Industrial Plastics in
Burbank, I saw you sitting in the lobby, lost in the rabbit-hole that
was their voluminous supply catalogue. You had SUCH a forlorn
expression on your face, (softy I am) could not resist trying to
help. Perhaps you remember?

I asked if I could be of some assistance? ... you said "Yes,
please," (a turning-point in history, at least for me) as you
explained that you were needing to engineer in an extreme saline
application. (WOW! MY SPECIALITY!) Together, we sat there
in instant collaborative friendship, and came up with the basic
circulation/pump & filtration system that I think got used in
some of the subsequent floatation tanks. Out of that chance/
cosmic encounter (and our cordial relationship over several years
thereafter) I went on to spend around one hundred hours floating
at your oasis of the Beverly Hills Center.

One evening, I stopped by to float and found that the
entire premises had been vacated! Everything had been moved
out, completely bare. The ONLY remaining indication that the
business ever even existed was the rectangular, carved/wooden
"Samadhi" sign on the parking lot wall, with its arrow that pointed
to the front door.

OK, maybe the removal of the sign had been hastily overlooked, but surely you would be back for it? So I returned a few
days later (with tools) and the apparently abandoned sign was still
there!

Figuring better saved as a precious memento of a wonderful
era than thrown away by new tenants, I detached the sign and took

it. It has been in safe-keeping, on precious display at my homes for all these many years.

Now, the quandary after decades is ... did I "save" it from the trash? ... or ... DID I STEAL IT?!?! The question to you & Glenn: Would you like your sign back?

We asked Gary for a photo for this piece and he sent the following email:

Greetings Glenn & Lee, SO nice to hear from you!
Attached is a (real) pix of me.
I am an artist, craftsman & inventor.
Sorry, do not have fancy pictures of m'self looking like a stock-broker or something.
D'best pix are of me doing what I do.
Don't have a camera, TV, wristwatch, or even a cellphone.
I DO however have my priorities straight.
So I DO have a fifty-five thousand dollar floatation laboratory in Hollywood that is d'most fab thing I could imagine.
(In Canada, under construction, is a one hundred thousand dollar ultimate "Sensorium" that is underground)
I still believe the whole sensory deprivation concept...
has the highest potential of anything going.

Michael Hutchison
By Shoshana Leibner

Michael Hutchison and I were friends for over 30 years. In the beginning it wasn't even clear how big of a role he would play in the world of floating, and, looking back, I am pleased to have known him and called him my friend.

Our first meeting: I brought him into the tank room and gave him an orientation. When he came out he sat in silence in the lobby for almost 4 hours, writing. I'd have a glimpse of him while taking care of other people and cleaning the rooms. We didn't chat much during his early floating but at some point, either weeks or months later, he became a permanent fixture in our center for a year. We started to talk about the meaning of things and the power of words, about the confusion of calling the float experience sensory deprivation. We'd laugh. We shared some type of synergy.

The Village Voice asked him to float to see if floating was a fad. He ended up writing an article a year later with a picture on the cover and for the centerfold. We were already booked twenty-four hours, six months in advance due to the movie *Altered States*. *The Village Voice* article helped to maintain a current buzz. At some point Michael told me he was going to write a book about floating so that my parents, Lee and Glenn Perry, would become famous and successful; so I would leave my boyfriend who owned Tranquility Tanks in Manhattan, and run off and live with Michael till the end of time. He wrote *The Book of Floating* in 1984.

Well, that's not how the story ended. Years later I got a call that his place had burned down. He told me he had lost twenty years of manuscripts when his computer burned. At the time I knew nothing about computers but by chance I asked a friend to go by his place in Santa Fe to see if they could find something called a hard drive. I heard that the hard drive was really hard to destroy and might be in the ashes. It was! Mike was forever grateful and I saved that twenty years of materials for him.

Then he had another accident where he fell off a bridge into an icy creek and broke his neck. He fell again and again and had to start from scratch to learn how to use his body. I purchased a voice activated computer so he could write, and stay in touch with people over Skype. Originally, *The Book of Floating* did not include anything about how he used the tank and what he thought about it. After he broke his neck and was immobilized for months, he found himself re-imagining his earlier floating experiences. In that meditative state he recreated a state of bliss which transformed his life outlook. [Editor's Note: "The Enlightenment Explanation," Chapter Twenty-six, *The Book of Floating*, Gateways Books, 3rd printing, 2017]

I did my best to be helpful until he died, in 2013. He was a great storyteller and I will forever miss him.

Floatation Center Accreditation
Why Accreditation?

There are several important reasons for an accreditation program. The first is to ensure quality for the floating public, and another is for the industry to monitor itself rather than be regulated by external authorities. Public bathing places such as pools, spas and floatation tank centers arc inspected by public health departments. These are city or county agencies overseeing public health and safety. Health departments have been ignorant of the requirements of floatation tanks, and in some cases set uninformed standards that prevented centers from functioning.

A new industry, through its official organization, can submit suggested regulatory standards to government agencies. If those standards are obviously designed to protect the health and safety of the public, there is a high probability they will be accepted. With our industry, we felt it most important that a set of standards be available for Public Health Authorities, to support and educate those wishing to establish businesses, and to support those who patronize these businesses in having the optimum experience.

With this in mind, the Board of Directors formulated the following set of guidelines.

Guidelines

Passed by F.T.A. Board of Directors

Since the purposes and functions of the Floatation Tank Association (hereinafter called "FTA") include the definition and promotion of ethical practices and the establishment of standards of safety and sanitation for commercial and professional floatation tank centers; and

Since it is in the best interest of the public and the floatation industry that the industry be self-monitoring rather than regulated by external authority; and

Since the floatation tank is an environment free from the distractions of light, sound, and gravity that affords one the maximum opportunity simply to be with oneself; and

Since the opportunity simply to be with oneself free of external distractions is intrinsically valuable; and

Since it is the interest of the FTA and its membership to promote conditions which maximally support the availability of that value to floaters; Now it is resolved that the FTA will certify as "Accredited by the Floatation Tank Association" members which agree to, and do, uphold the following criteria:

For Commercial Center Accreditation

I. The fundamental priority of the floatation center be that it serves the floater, rather than sells floating. Floaters shall not be exposed to pressure sales tactics or be approached in any manner that imposes on the floater's experience, sanctuary or choice.

2. The center will maintain an environment that is sensitive to and supportive of the floater's experience:

a) a quiet room or area will be provided for floaters before and after using the tank.

b) the floater's right to interact minimally or maximally with staff will be respected. Staff will be sensitive to the floater's responses when entering and leaving the tank and will recognize and respect the validity of each person's experience.

c) the floater's privacy will be insured by the environment. (One tank to a room, one person using bathroom at any time.)

d) first-time floaters will receive a clear and thorough orientation prior to floating.

e) the first three floats will be without audio or video, in order to insure, the right of the floater to discover what it is like to be with him or herself in the environment.

f) the end of the float session will be signaled in a gentle way consistent with the experience and insuring the floater's privacy.

3. Consistent with providing the optimum environment for the float experience, the center will observe the following criteria for cleanliness and sanitation:

a) clean tank rooms and bathrooms will be provided and maintained between uses.

b) the entire volume of tank water will he filtered between uses and the level of H_2O will be checked daily,

c) condition of water and tank will be monitored between uses.

d) clean towels and toiletries will be provided for floater's use and comfort,

e) only one floater will be permitted to use the tank and shower facilities at any time.

f) temperature of water will be checked between uses.

g) PH will be checked and recorded at least bi-monthly and the acceptable range is 7.2 to 7.6

h) specific gravity will be checked and recorded at least twice weekly and the acceptable range is 1.24 to 1.27.

1) tank water will be tested for purity by a certified outside laboratory or Board of Health on a regular basis.

j) the inside of the tank above the solution line will be cleaned weekly or more often if necessary.

k) weekly tank maintenance procedures will include the use of chemicals such as bromine or chlorine to keep bacteria at safe and acceptable levels. Tanks using ultraviolet irradiation of water may not be required to use chemicals if testing of the water by outside lab shows acceptable bacteria levels.

4. Moral and Ethical Considerations Accredited tank centers

a) refrain from urging people to buy products and do not exert undue pressure for the purchase of additional floats.

b) refrain from making inflated claims about the benefits of floatation both in advertising and public statement.   c) refuse use of the tank to anyone who is intoxicated or "high" on drugs; to epileptics not under medication, and to anyone who has a communicable disease.

d) refuse to float two people in the same tank at the same time.

e) give a clear and complete orientation to first time floaters before they enter the tank.

These guidelines were presented to the FTA membership in 1985 and resulted in a great deal of discussion on the pros and cons. The membership was offered the opportunity to make alternate proposals and none were offered.

Although these guidelines were passed by the Board of Directors, they were never implemented. The following are the implementation items in the guidelines:

f) publicly display the FTA Accreditation Certificate

g) have on hand and furnish to floaters upon request FTA's Guidelines of Accreditation

h) cooperate with FTA in verifying compliance with all criteria

i) include this statement on their floater registration form:

"This center is accredited by the Floatation Tank Association (FTA) as verified by the posted certificate. The FTA manual of Floatation Center Accreditation is available here for inspection, and a copy of the Guidelines for Accreditation is available to you upon request."

There is an additional guideline for Professional Centers - those which apply floating in support of other specific professional services:

First-time floaters will be given a clear and complete orientation before their first float which will include addressing fears that could obstruct or impinge on their experience of floating for the first time. The practitioner will explain to the floater that the first float will be free of any influence, activity or input, such as audio or video, that would prevent a direct experience of floating for the purpose of allowing the person to adjust to the tank.

Requests for these guidelines have been escalating recently. They are published here to inform everyone of their existence, and to encourage discussion of this vital matter. The first article was submitted by Dr. Dantes. Your articles are invited.

The Original Floating Experience: Holding Open The Possibility

In this article I would like to explore with you the unique importance of the floater's introduction to the original floating experience—how that introduction determines whether or not possibilities valuable to first-time floaters are preserved, and how preserving those possibilities relates to the accreditation of floatation centers.

As a floater and long-time supporter of the floating industry, I had the great privilege of participating with the Floatation Tank Association (FTA) Board of Directors when it was creating the "Guidelines for Accreditation of Floatation Centers." The Guidelines represent the best work of people who came together to share and contribute from their knowledge and their life experience—to benefit floaters and floating. Many of these people are the pioneers in the field of floating, among them Dr. John C. Lilly. The purpose of the "Guidelines for Accreditation" is to establish and maintain standards, concerning every aspect of the operation of a floatation center, in order to promote the value and benefit of floating. Clearly, what benefits floating also benefits the floating industry.

One of the guidelines, especially, is deserving of special attention, as it is basic to the original floating experience. The guideline is that a commercial floatation center will assure that the floater's introductory experience to floating is free of any added input—audio or video—except for music gently signalling the end of the float. The first three floats will be free of any added input; after that it is up to the floater's discretion to float with or without added input. The aim of this article is to examine how floating freely (without added input) is vital in the floater's introduction to the experience of floating.

Let's begin by considering, together, what the floating environment is. A floatation tank is a light-proof, sound-proof, gravity-free environment into which one enters, lays back and floats —instantly, effortlessly, due to the buoyancy of the water. What is such an environment? In simple terms, it is an environment in which nothing is happening. Is such an environment good for something? We could start by acknowledging that the floating environment is, to begin with, good for nothing. And what is nothing good for?

We know that people in other cultures have, for centuries, engaged in practices such as yoga and meditation, in order to transcend physical and mental phenomena, and realize the original state of consciousness in which nothing is happening. And in this modern age, the same state of inner peace and clarity is available to people in our culture through the floating experience. Floating, which is effortless, essentially eliminates "practicing" at transcending. There is nothing to learn, nothing to do. Upon being in the floating environment, the body relaxes completely, the mind releases, and the consciousness is free to be in its original state, like a clear sky. The floating environment, where nothing is happening, is designed perfectly to support and facilitate a basically natural state (and that is the nature of the original floating experience, which is basically something about nothing). The rest, relaxation, rejuvenation is so profound, that the floating experience is like taking a vacation in an hour! Now, let's consider what else is available from floating, beyond transcendence.

Floating freely without distraction, when the mind and body are transcended, it is possible to make the simple enquiry: What is consciousness in its original state? This question opens the field of subtle distinction, the field of self-exploration, of self-discovery. Consciousness beyond mind and body is capable of distinguishing new possibilities, unlimited possibilities, which are not based on something, but which are distinguished into existence, out of nothing itself. This field is not infringed on by the mentality or reality which has already been released—an advantage to exploring this field of possibility. We are referring to the field of original creativity. I myself have experienced this, floating, when nothing is happening, and everything's possible, or something could be made of it.

Coming out of the floating experience, one re-enters one's mental and material embodiment gradually, sensitively. And if one chooses to act on the opportunity offered by some from newly-discovered possibility, one could make it a reality, having just made up something from nothing. This is a possible way that floating could be used, amongst others (such as experiential, educational, therapeutic) but one certainly worthy of preserving, for first-time floaters.

How does this relate to the accreditation guideline that the floater's introduction to the original floating experience will be free of added input? The release which is transcendence, the exploration of self-distinction, self-discovery, or creativity which we have been discussing, require an environment where nothing is happening. These are subtle functions, which for most of us are easily overshadowed by the stimuli of sight, sound, and sensational input — in short, sensory overload (which is exactly what the tank was originally designed to relieve us from. And since then there have been additional experiences added, in various forms).

The floater's introduction to the floating environment, the original experience of floating, is when the floater experientially develops the first impressions of what floating is. Like the first time for almost everything, it is never exactly the same again. If the floater is deprived of the opportunity to experience that nothing is happening originally, and begins associating floating with specialized usages (where something is happening), it is questionable that the experience that nothing is happening, and the field of subtle distinction, will ever be available to the floater again—and that would be a serious disservice to the floater.

As a common analogy, consider the experience of tasting a fine dish. If the original dish is presented without adding anything, a person has both options—the spiced and unspiced version, and can add spice according to taste. However, if the first experience is the spiced version, it is doubtful that the original version would even be tasted, let alone appreciated. Variety is the spice of life. We want to hold open the possibility.

To preserve the original experience of floating, the FTA has produced a guideline to accredit floatation centers which introduce the floater to the floating environment in its original state. After that, additional accessories are also available, at the floater's choice. This holds open the possibility.

It has been an honor to consider this subject with you. Thank you for the opportunity.

David Dantes, M.D. is a certified specialist in Emergency Medicine, caring for patients at trauma centers, and an assistant Professor at UCLA School of Medicine. He also is an explorer of consciousness, as a floater for the last six years.

Our Orientation

For safety, a proper orientation needs to be provided to everyone before their first float. It needs to be given verbally, with sufficient presence, so that it is fully understood.

I am going to talk to you about the tank for a few minutes. I will include the things we have found most people want to know before their first float.

Many people have some fear or concern before they use the tank the first time, fears such as being alone in the dark, drowning, not having enough air, claustrophobia, and others.

The fears are usually based on the thought or the idea that you will not be in control of the situation. In this situation, you are totally in control. During your session you can get in and out of the tank any time you want.

There is no particular way to use the tank that is more correct than another. Any way you use it is correct, as long as it is comfortable for you.

The first thing to do before your first float is to open the door. Note that it is very easy to open.

You can use the tank with the door completely open, you can keep it partially open with your towel, or you can close it. When you get into any tank, open and close the door several times before you lie down to get the feel of it. Also prior to lying down, feel the area around the door and the door itself, both with your eyes open and closed, so you are clear how to find the door if you are in the tank without light and want to find the door easily.

The tank is designed so that it is not airtight. You will have plenty of air. To keep the tank air fresher, an air circulation system brings additional air in from the room.

The tank environment is humid.

There are ten inches of water in the tank with hundreds of pounds of epsom salt dissolved in it. The salt makes the solution so dense that when you lie back you will float like a cork. Your ears will be underwater. There are earplugs available if you would like them, and we recommend them if you have ever had ear problems. If you would like some earplugs, ask for them. They do not help minimize sound.

You can experiment with the best body position for you. For example: hands behind head, on your chest, along your sides. If you have tension in your neck you can relieve it by clasping your hands behind your head or by using a head float.

If you get any solution in your eyes you will be uncomfortable for a few minutes. To avoid getting solution in your eyes, push your hair back on your forehead when you change from lying down to sitting up. Also, keep your salty hands away from your face. If you do happen to get salt in your eyes, have your towel just outside the door where you can easily reach it, and use it to wipe your eyes.

If you have cuts or scratches or have recently shaved, there may be stinging for several minutes. If you have any open cuts use liquid bandage to seal them.

Remove your metal jewelry and contact lenses. Shower, shampoo, rinse thoroughly and dry your face. Then get into the tank.

At the end of your float, a signal will let you know your time is up. Move slowly. Sit up, open the door, stand and squeegee the solution from your body before getting out of the tank. Step directly in front of the tank.

Then shower and shampoo the salt off well before doing anything else. After you dress, the bathroom has the amenities you need.

If the tank solution is too warm or the air too stuffy to be comfortable, put your towel in the door. Do not use the tank when you are too warm.

Enjoy your float and check with your guide for any additional information.

Samadhi Philosophy

We recognize our obligation to make ourselves available to people after their use of the tank, whether we provide silence, another appointment, good listening and good responding, or something we haven't thought of. We are there to listen and help them explore their experience, if that's what they're interested in doing. We realize that we best serve our customers and ourselves by reflecting truthfully, in our own behavior, the fundamental, positive qualities of the tank experience itself. Our job is to remain open-minded, unbiased, centered, supportive, relaxed, personally responsible and energetically aware. Really working in this way keeps our work a source of personal growth and evolution.

The tank is a general-purpose tool, not a design for something in particular. It is nothing and it is a powerful instrument for change. It is an environment for learning about oneself, in whatever way one wishes, without distraction. It does not tell us what to do, and neither should we presume to tell others what their experience should be, either before or after their float. We trust in the inherent capacity of the individual to discover what is best for themselves. We believe that the most effective experience occurs when initiative and power is left with the person and we are there to encourage that. After floating, people are often in the present moment, and emit the glow of present time unfolding, a sense of peace and wellbeing. When we welcome this state, it may be eager to make a return visit on following floats.

A Question of Time

On the website Peak Prosperity, I read a scary story written by
Dr. Albert Bartlett, a University of Colorado Physics Professor.
It illustrates that the power of compounding and exponential
growth invariably leads to the impending depletion of our earth's
resources: plant, mineral and animal.

*Imagine you are in a huge waterproof stadium, perhaps the
Miami Marlins' domed baseball stadium. You are handcuffed to a
top bleacher, and suspended from the center of the ceiling is a magic
dropper.*

*The dropper starts by putting out one drop, and each minute it
drops twice what it did the minute before. The first minute, it does one
drop; the second, two drops; the third, four drops; the fourth, eight;
and so on. If we start at 11AM, how soon do we have to get freed? Is
it a day, week, month, year? It is fifty minutes. That is, ten minutes to
noon.*

*How full is it at eleven minutes until noon? Half. And at twelve
minutes until noon? One-quarter. At thirteen minutes until noon, it
would be one-eighth full. When the stadium is only five feet full, you
only have five minutes left. The important takeaway is that by the
time we understand the situation it is often too late. This demonstrates
the power of compounding. When something grows over time, such as
population and demand for oil – anything that steadily increases in
size through a consistent time period – and you graph it over time, the
graph will look like a hockey stick.*

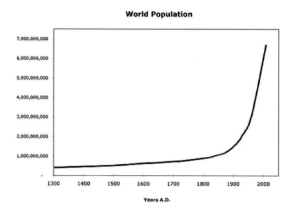

We are feeling the effects of the compounding growth in our production of garbage, topsoil depletion, and energy demand. This fuels climate change, the depletion of natural resources, and native plants and animals. We live on a very limited planet except the trash. We seem to have an unlimited amount of that. And of course, the amount of it is also exponential. Though we practice recycling, in addition to other problems, most processing is way too difficult to do well. Due to the contamination in recycled plastic, within the last few years, Samadhi has experienced five to ten times as many manufactured part failures as we had in the previous thirty-five.

Interconnectedness results in many more things having an effect on the process. Events will move much faster than most people expect. Think about the weather getting twice as bad as the previous time period, and the time period is less than five years, well.

I have been dealing with how I mentally, emotionally and spiritually deal with this problem. And in my moments of clarity, I think that everything is God and is going as planned and everything is in balance. It does not mean I do not do whatever I can to remedy the situation such as farming biodynamically without tilling, and being mindful of our waste stream. It just means I do not freak-out; I do not add my emotional negativity to the situation. As I mentioned at the end of our part of the Why Float chapter, I can work to manifest the consciousness I want by experiencing it as already present, feeling blessed that I experience it, and maintain that.

Remembering what Franklin D. Roosevelt said in his first inaugural address "Let me assert my firm belief that the only thing we have to fear is...fear itself." What I have found to be the most help is "A Verse for Our Time" on the next page.

Over one hundred years ago Rudolf Steiner wrote:

A Verse for Our Time

We must eradicate from the soul
All fear and terror of what comes towards man out of the future.

We must acquire serenity
In all feelings and sensations about the future.

We must look forward with absolute equanimity
To everything that may come.

And we must think only that whatever comes
Is given to us by a world-directive full of wisdom.

It is part of what we must learn in this age,
namely, to live out of pure trust,
Without any security in existence.

Trust in the ever-present help
Of the spiritual world.

Truly, nothing else will do
If our courage is not to fail us.

And let us seek the awakening from within ourselves,
every morning and every evening.

Recommended Information

Cowan, Thomas S, MD, Sally Fallon Morell. *The Contagion Myth: Why Viruses (including "Coronavirus") Are Not the Cause of Disease.* **NY, NY: Skyhorse Publishing. 2020.**

The most important book I ever read. Get it from the author here: https://drtomcowan.com/. It is so important it was censored by the largest bookseller. If you have any health conditions, read all of Dr. Thomas S. Cowan books. Often one about a particular topic has important information about other conditions. Probably the most wide-ranging one is the one listed above. He has written significant books about the heart, cancer, child and baby care, healing and vaccines.

Fallon Morell, Sally, Mary G. Enig, PhD. *Nourishing Traditions: The Cookbook That Challenges Politically Correct Nutrition and the Diet Dictocrats.* **Brandywine, MD. 2000.**

I consider this the best dietary book and is both a cookbook and a book about nutrition and health. Great information on the Weston A Price Foundation website including their brochure here: https://www.westonaprice.org/health-topics/abcs-of-nutrition/ principles-of-healthy-diets-2/ Follow this for the best health.

Firstenberg, Arthur. The Invisible Rainbow: A History of Electricity and Life. Sante Fe, NM: AGB Press. 2020.

The Contagion Myth, mentioned above, may run into strong programs we have. Reading this helped me dissolve them.

Kiss the Ground. Producers: Benenson Productions, Big Picture Ranch, The Redford Center. Distributor: Netflix (2020)
"Narrated and featuring Woody Harrelson, Kiss the Ground is an inspiring and groundbreaking film that reveals the first viable solution to our climate crisis. Kiss the Ground reveals that, by regenerating the world's soils, we can completely and rapidly stabilize Earth's climate, restore lost ecosystems and create abundant food supplies. Using compelling graphics and visuals, along with striking NASA and NOAA footage, the film artfully

illustrates how, by drawing down atmospheric carbon, soil is the missing piece of the climate puzzle."

Lilly, John C. Dr., E. J. Gold. Tanks for the Memories: Floatation Tank Talks. Nevada City, CA: Gateways Books & Tapes, 1985.
This book is not for the beginning floater. If you are very serious about working on yourself, it can be very useful.

Anything by Dr. John C. Lilly, especially: T*he Deep Self; Center of the Cyclone; Programming and Metaprogramming in the Human Biocomputer; Simulations of God;* and, *The Science of Belief.*

Anything by E.J. Gold, especially: *American Book of the Dead; The Human Biological Machine as a Transformational Apparatus; Practical Work on Self;* and *Parallel Worlds Explored.*
See https://www.idhhb.com/.

Goleman, Daniel, Richard Davidson. *Altered Traits: Science Reveals How Meditation Changes Your Mind, Brain, and Body.* New York City: Avery Publishing Group, 2017.
Choosing the highest quality research studies, the authors demonstrate the crucial ingredients necessary for the lasting personality traits that a meditation practice can offer, and how quickly results may appear.

Karim, Dr. Ibrahim, Back To a Future for Mankind: BioGeometry. Egypt: BioGeometry Consulting Ltd, Dr. Ibrahim F. Karim, 2010.
Generally, it is thought that form follows function. Dr. Ibrahim shows that, in the Universe, function follows form.

Lovel, Hugh. Quantum Agriculture: Biodynamics and Beyond. Blairsville, GA: Quantum Agriculture Publishers, 2014.
An excellent book, from a good friend and floater, on Biodynamics and much other useful gardening/ farming information.

Young, Shinzen. *The Science of Enlightenment: How Meditation Works. Boulder, CO: Sounds True. 2016, 2018.*
A clear, concise and simple explanation of how meditation and enlightenment work. It is accessible and profoundly useful, making both science and spiritual matters available to all. He brings in practices from all religions and shows how alike they are. It is the best piece I have read for why to meditate or float; bound to be a classic for many years.

Coincidentally, we have a long history with Shinzen Young. He reports: In the 1980s, the Samadhi Tank group graciously allowed me and my students access to their Beverly Hills floating facility after hours. I'd take a group of ten students and we'd meditate all night, alternating two hour blocks in the tank with two hour blocks of seated practice. In Buddhism, there's a concept of upaya--"expedient means." We found that applying systematic focus techniques during long floats could serve as an upaya, facilitating certain aspects of the practice.
—November 2020. Shinzen Young, Co-Director, SEMA Lab, University of Arizona.

Acres, U.S.A.
A great magazine for growing anything and learning about how the world works. https://www.acresusa.com/
Everyone can grow food even if it is only one pot. Go to our website to get more information about many subjects including gardening: https://www.samadhitank.com/index.html

There is lots more to see on the Samadhi website and if you have anything to share, send it to us.

Contact Information

GATEWAYS BOOKS & TAPES
P.O. BOX 370
NEVADA CITY, CA 95959
PHONE: (530) 271-2239 OR (800) 869-0658
EMAIL: INFO@GATEWAYSBOOKSANDTAPES.COM
www.gatewaysbooksandtapes.com

Gateways Floating Books Distributed by:
Independent Publishers Group (IPG)
Chicago, Illinois
Customer Service: (312) 337-0747

Note: If you are going to order books in wholesale quantities, we
recommend that for any location east of the Rocky Mountains
or in Canada, you set up a wholesale account and order direct
from IPG—just tell them Iven Lourie referred you to stock up on
floating books. They will give you a good discount and treat you
very well!

SAMADHI TANK COMPANY
LEE AND GLENN PERRY
WWW.SAMADHITANK.COM
PHONE: (530) 477-1319
EMAIL: LEE@SAMADHITANK.COM